THE WIDOW OF BORLEY

The Widow of Borley

a psychical investigation

Robert Wood

Duckworth

First published in 1992
Gerald Duckworth & Co. Ltd.,
The Old Piano Factory
48 Hoxton Square, London N1 6PB

A catalogue record for this book is available
from the British Library

ISBN 0 7156 2419 9

Photoset in North Wales by
Derek Doyle & Associates, Mold, Clwyd.
Printed in Great Britain by
WBC Print Ltd, Bridgend, Glamorgan.

Contents

Plates

Plates 1-8 are reproduced by courtesy of the Harry Price Library, University of London.

Preface

Although much of the material in this book is the result of my own investigation into the life of Marianne Foyster and her role in the haunting of Borley Rectory, Essex, in the 1930s, I have drawn heavily on the work of the late Trevor Hall. Without Hall, who tracked Marianne down in the mid-1950s when her confusing trail was still warm, this book would not have been written.

Many people have helped me in piecing together this complex story. I offer special thanks to Alan Wesencraft of the Harry Price Library of the University of London, who not only gave me permission to use the collection of original material on the alleged haunting of Borley, but who also freely offered patient guidance and much-needed advice. I also thank the University of London Library for granting permission for the reproduction of original material from the Harry Price collection in this book.

John Fisher, Marianne's adopted son, has helped me with his memories of his early days, and by allowing me to read Marianne's letters to him.

Mr Harvey Malmberg, Archivist of the Diocese of New Brunswick, and Ms Twila Buttimer, Archivist of New Brunswick, assisted me by tracking down the parish records relating to Marianne's second husband, the Reverend Lionel Algernon Foyster.

I should also like to thank the Secretary and Librarian of Pembroke College, Cambridge, the staff of Kensington and Chelsea public libraries, the staff of the public libraries in Jamestown and Fargo, North Dakota, and Cory Jonson of VFW Post #762, Fargo.

R.W.

Introduction

In 1946 Harry Price, the self-styled psychical investigator (he liked to call himself a 'psychist'), whose sensational, pseudo-scientific reports of his alleged encounters with the supernatural had turned him into an international celebrity, published *The End of Borley Rectory*, the second of his best-selling books about the alleged haunting of Borley Rectory in Essex, and a sequel to his *The Most Haunted House in England*. In August of the same year a liner arrived in New York harbour carrying a forty-six-year-old Englishwoman for whom the publication of Price's books was a disaster, for they resulted in her being pursued for the next forty years by psychical investigators, private detectives, assorted charlatans and sensation-seekers. She started her new but shadowed life on a farm near Hokah, a small town in the Mississippi bluff country of Minnesota, and began to move restlessly through the American heartlands, to Jamestown in North Dakota as a newspaper reporter, to Fargo as first a 'special instructor' at an agricultural college and then a social worker with the Lutheran Welfare Service, and finally back to the Mississippi to La Crosse in Wisconsin, where she still lives.

This woman was Marianne, the subject of this biography. She has used many names throughout her long life, but when she arrived in New York she was Marianne O'Neil, one of 'Eisenhower's Sweethearts', as the British GI brides were called. No doubt many British women crossed the Atlantic to join the men they truly loved, although wartime shortages, inconvenient pregnancies, and tales of abundant T-bone steaks, large cars and wonderful skyscrapers perhaps played some part; yet of all the women who left the British Isles during this period none could have had more pressing, or more unusual, reasons for doing so than Marianne.

Although Marianne's character and way of life have been extraordinary by any standards, she would have escaped the attentions of the relentless psychical researchers and their camp followers if she had not spent five years, from October 1930 to October 1935, at Borley Rectory as the wife of the then Rector, the Reverend Lionel Algernon Foyster. At Borley Marianne claimed to have witnessed wonders that are still widely regarded as among the most convincing examples of poltergeist activity ever recorded. As she said, 'What sets out as a bit of fun can surely get one into a lot of trouble.' Her claims were publicised by Price, and this publicity eventually involved her not only in more or less continuous harassment for the rest of her life, but also in revelations about her other activities which involve fraud on a truly incredible scale, blackmail, adultery and bigamy, and even allegations that she was a murderess possessed of supernatural powers.

This book is not about psychical research; it is about Marianne. But because of Marianne's own claims, and because of her long association with psychical researchers, events which have been interpreted as supernatural intervention in human affairs, and the integrity, motives and methods of those who choose to study and publicise such matters will have to be considered. It is important to emphasise that in this book I do not present a general case either for or against the reality of poltergeist activities or other supernatural agents. I believe, however, that there is compelling evidence to suggest that Marianne's claims were wholly fraudulent and that the entire Borley haunting, including the cult that persists to this day, is based on nothing more than unscrupulous sensation-seeking on the one hand and credulity on the other.

It is a sad commentary on the mentality of self-styled psychical researchers that they will minutely examine Marianne's accounts of the wonders she once claimed to have seen while ignoring her complex psychopathology and the unusual domestic situation at the Rectory that undoubtedly led her to make these claims. A large popular literature exists on Borley and Marianne; the style of these works hovers uneasily between Conan Doyle and *The Boy's Own Paper*, and the authors invariably refer to themselves as 'trained and serious investigators', though they never make clear where they received their training and do not identify the frivolous investigators with whom they do not wish to be confused. These authors also display a peculiar mixture of snobbery and naivety when, while adducing testimony of the wonders observed at Borley, they refer to Marianne's husband the Rector as 'a cultured and intelligent observer', on the strength, one assumes, of his being a Cambridge graduate and a country parson. Obviously a Cambridge graduate and a country parson would never claim to have witnessed supernatural marvels if he had not really done so. Such an attitude precludes an intelligent interpretation of what happened at Borley, and of the subsequent careers of the Rector and his wife. Even Trevor Hall, the one author and investigator who acknowledged that Marianne was not only a fraud but a pathological liar with a complex personality, could not bring himself to believe that her husband was anything more than a helpless dupe who grudgingly cooperated with his wife's deceptions and impostures because he had no choice. Hall had a boundless respect for Cambridge, expressed in his own fantasy that he was a Cambridge graduate himself, which he wasn't.

No sense can be made of the story of the Rector and his wife unless it is admitted that he had as peculiar a sexuality as his wife, and that he too was prepared to fantasise and deceive regardless of the calamitous consequences it might have for the miserable people with whom they became involved. Most of the writers on the wonders of Borley seem able to accept the theory that the house was haunted by the ghost of a French nun who displaced a French-English dictionary in the nineteenth century, so that she could master sufficient English to scribble strange messages on the Rectory walls in the twentieth century, asking for 'light mass, and prayers', and yet cannot bring themselves to believe that a country parson who was also a Cambridge graduate was also a sexual deviant and a liar. The inevitable conclusion is that most writers on Borley are either rather dim or deliberately persist in distorting or ignoring the known facts to keep their bandwagon rolling.

*

I grew up in a small village only a few miles from Borley, and I well remember childhood excursions to 'see the ghosts'. I never saw any, not even the nun perusing her borrowed dictionary. I never saw the Rectory either, because it was burned down in 1939 by the then owner, one Capt. Gregson RE (retired), in order to obtain the fire-insurance money. Yet many of the popular books on Borley and its ghosts, while acknowledging that the Captain was a dubious fellow, persist in relating how the Rectory *might* have been burned down by an 'entity' named Sunex Amures, who, for reasons known only to himself and his astral confederates, chose to reveal his identity and his nefarious intentions during an amateur seance in Streatham; while certain authors are happy to recount this rollicking yarn, they are coy about quoting the professional judgment of Mr (later Sir) William Crocker, a lawyer representing the insurance company, and the loss adjuster, the redoubtable Col. Cuthbert Buckle, which was expressed as follows: 'We repudiated his [i.e. Gregson's] impudent claim for "accidental loss by fire" – £7,356 – pleading bluntly that he had fired the place himself.'

But Capt. Gregson's interesting experiment with arson and bogus fire-insurance claims, which left the Rectory gutted, was not the first attempt by a resident of the house to plumb the depths of human credulity. Marianne had been there before him; and while Gregson was trying to perpetrate a cheap and shabby fraud, Marianne's motives were much more interesting; and so were those of that country parson and Cambridge graduate, her husband the Rev. Lionel Algernon, who faithfully recorded his wife's experiences in his diary and later tried to turn them into a best-selling thriller. None the less the story of Capt. Gregson and the fiery 'entity' Sunex Amures puts the Borley cult in its proper context; it is absurd. Yet behind the tale of the haunting, and largely ignored by the professional psychical researchers, is the fascinating tale of Marianne and her husband.

Inevitably this book will be read by some enthusiasts of the Borley cult; and for their benefit I end this introduction with a few words about the value of first-hand testimony of supposed supernatural marvels.

Two points are worth making. The first is that psychical researchers seem to have great difficulty discriminating between an experience and its interpretation. The second is that many of them appear to have no idea what constitutes proof. The first point can be illustrated by considering accounts of UFOs. To claim to have seen an unidentified flying object is one thing; to claim that this object was a flying saucer is quite another. In the context of the alleged haunting of Borley it is not at all marvellous that four sisters saw a figure they couldn't identify in the Rectory garden one evening in the summer of 1900; to claim that they saw the ghost of a murdered French nun is fantastic.

The very vocabulary used by many writers on Borley prejudges the issue, because the event and the supposed agent are confused. Footsteps of an unseen person become the footsteps of invisible feet, a coat is touched by an 'unseen hand', the movements of household objects are said, without further explanation of examination and possible causes, to 'defy rational explanation'. The interesting implication of this is that such authors therefore feel free to indulge in irrationality at length and without restraint.

The second point, that of what may be held to constitute proof, is also illustrated by the story of the nun in the garden, which is one of the tales upon which the Borley legend is based, and of which Marianne made use for her own peculiar ends. It is not enough to state that four people saw a ghost and then leave the sceptics to disprove it. It *cannot* be disproved. The burden of proof lies squarely on the shoulders of those who claim to see ghosts, to hear footsteps from invisible feet, and to detect movements for which they can find no rational explanation. Shifting the burden of proof is one of the oldest tricks of the peddlars of supernatural marvels; and I do not intend to waste time in this book by falling into the trap.

Behind the Borley legend, which, according to taste can be

considered picturesque or absurd, lies the far more interesting, and true, tale of that sinister couple, Lionel Algernon and his wife – Marianne.

**GHOST VISITS TO
A RECTORY**

Tales of Headless Coachmen
and a Lonely Nun

THE ELOPERS

Mysterious Happenings on Site
of Old Monastery

1

Borley Rectory and its Ghosts

Borley lies on the western shoulder of the valley of the River Stour, about two miles from the market town of Sudbury, and about the same distance from the large village of Long Melford. Here the river forms the boundary between the counties of Suffolk and Essex, with Borley lying on the Essex side. Borley itself can hardly be graced with the title of a hamlet, for apart from the church (a medieval building, of unknown dedication), a country house named Borley Place, a few modern buildings on the site of the Rectory, the old Rectory cottage and some scattered cottages and farm-houses, there is nothing: no shop, no pub, no post-office. Borley has not suffered the fate of other English villages since the war; it was always tiny and remote. Sixty years ago, when the Foysters arrived, it must have been much the same as it is now, except that the Rectory was still standing and Long Melford station, which was closer to Borley than to the village whose name it bore, provided an escape route to Bury St Edmunds, Colchester, Ipswich and, of course, London. In the 1933 edition of *Crockford's*, the population of Borley is given as 137 souls.

I mentioned in the introduction that I spent my childhood a few miles from Borley, in the nearby Suffolk village of Acton, and was quite familiar with the story of the ghost. I remember meeting people who claimed to have seen the Borley ghost, or ghosts, and a man who claimed to have seen the mysterious dark figures who appeared at the windows when the Rectory was on fire. This region of the border between Essex and Suffolk

abounds in ghost stories, and the original Borley legend was
unremarkable and typical of the genre.

A ghostly nun was said to perambulate in the Rectory garden
along a certain path that was picturesquely called 'The Nun's
Walk', in the lane between the Rectory and the Church, and in
the churchyard itself. Sometimes ghostly singing was said to
come from the Church itself during, of course, the hours of
darkness. The nun of Borley was not alone. She had company, of
a kind, in the form of a ghastly spectral coach, which usually
appeared at night, careering up the narrow lane that runs up
the hill from the main Sudbury-to-Long-Melford road and
through Borley. Sometimes the coach swerved through the
Rectory gates before vanishing into thin air, and sometimes it
swerved into a convenient hedge. Sometimes it would be driven
by a headless coachman, sometimes by two. Sometimes it
wouldn't appear at all, and be sensible to mortals only through
its grinding wheels and the pounding hooves of its straining
horses.

It is curious that none of the psychical researchers who have
written about Borley seem interested in patterns of local
folklore. In the village in which I spent my childhood an almost
identical story was told. A death-coach, driven by a headless
coachman (of course), pounded down a narrow lane and
vanished into the gates of the ruined Acton Place, once the home
of the famous eighteenth-century miser Robert Jennens, who
was the richest man in England but who chose to live in his
cellar, dressed in rags.

The death-coach is a psychopomp; Old Nick's emissaries have
come to take away the soul of a disturbing and scary person – in
this case, the notorious miser. Death-coach legends often grow
up around the houses and estates of men and women who were
feared and dreaded by the locals. Many writers on Borley relate
being told, by apparently sane and sober witnesses, how the
death-coach appeard to them during visits to Borley. They could
have heard exactly the same stories in nearby Acton, but did not
take the trouble to listen to them because Harry Price has not
made the village famous as the site of a haunting. We must
conclude either that these sightings of death-coaches are not to

be taken at face value, or that the lanes of the Suffolk-Essex border are congested with phantom horse-drawn conveyances which render driving after dark quite inadvisable.

The death-coach of Borley and the legend of the phantom nun were conflated into a romantic but absurd and anachronistic tale in which the nun was the shade of a young woman who had attempted to elope with a man described variously as a monk, a lay-brother and a groom from 'Borley Monastery'. There is no record of any monastic building at Borley, and even the most credulous ghost-hunters should surely be put on their guard by the stories of an underground tunnel that was said to connect the non-existent 'Borley Monastery' with the nun's convent at Bures, a village which is eight miles away.

According to the story, the couple, eloping in the coach (there were no such things as coaches before the English Reformation), were caught, and the monk was executed and the nun walled up in her convent. There is no evidence that such terrible punishments were dealt to religious who broke their vows. A variation on this theme has the monk, lay-brother or groom falling out with the nun during the elopement and strangling her, for which crime he was executed. And so on.

Borley Rectory was not an ancient building. It was built in 1863 by the then Rector of the parish, the Rev. Henry Dawson Ellis Bull, son of the Rev. Edward Bull of nearby Pentlow. The Bulls were one of those ecclesiastical dynasties that were such a prominent feature of English social life during the nineteenth and early twentieth centuries. According to the *Alumni Cantabrigienses*, the founder of the dynasty was John Bull, who was admitted to Christ's College, Cambridge, as a sizar in 1752, and who was at some time chaplain to the Earl of Macclesfield. John Bull was Rector of Pentlow from 1756 until his death in 1802. He was succeeded by his son John, who had also been to Christ's, and who was Rector of the parish from 1802 until his death in 1834. The second John was succeeded by *his* son Edward, who is recorded as having been admitted as a sizar at St John's College, Cambridge, on 4 November 1831. Edward Bull was Rector of Pentlow from 1834 until his death in 1877.

Edward Bull built a magnificent folly at Pentlow – 'Bull's

Tower', an octagonal, crenellated structure some sixty feet high. I remember the awe and wonder this inspired during my childhood, and the stories that were told about it by the local people; some said that 'Old Bull' had built it so that he could stand up there and watch people at work in the fields to ensure that no one shirked, others that he built it because he wanted to see the sea, but was very disappointed when it was finished because he couldn't, not even from the very top. In fact the tower was built in 1858 as a memorial to Edward Bull's parents.

Edward Bull had two clergyman sons: Henry Dawson Ellis Bull and Felix Edward Pepys Bull. The former, who was his heir, was born in 1833 and educated at Wadham College, Oxford, thus breaking the family's Cambridge tradition. The Rev. H.D.E. Bull also branched out on his own ecclesiastically, by taking the living of Borley and building a new Rectory for his growing family. His younger brother, the Rev. Felix Bull, became Rector of Pentlow, which living he held from 1877 to 1927.

The Rev. H.D.E. Bull's new Rectory was a red-brick monstrosity with high-gabled roofs and a peculiar tower over the front door. It was surrounded by high, gloomy trees and was, in the words of the insurance company's lawyer, William Crocker, 'as ugly as the bad taste of 1863 could make it'. The ground floor included large dining and drawing rooms looking out over the lawns, a library, a butler's pantry, a sewing room, a large kitchen, a larder, a dairy and a scullery. Upstairs on the first floor were eleven rooms including bedrooms, the bathroom and the lavatory. There were also a large attic and extensive cellars.

Bull had fourteen children, and in 1875-6 was obliged to add another wing to the house. The floor plans given on pp. 12-13 show that this almost enclosed the courtyard, leaving only a narrow gap between the end of the new wing and the scullery and bedroom of the old one. This is said to have given rise to curious acoustic effects which have been attributed to supernatural causes. The same plans also show that there were three staircases between the ground and first floors, the back stairs for the staff, the service stairs and the main staircase in the hall. If someone wanted to play at ghosts and move round the house quietly, it would have been very easy. The Rectory ended up as a sprawling rabbit-warren of a place, still surrounded by high, gloomy trees; from contemporary photographs (see Plate 1), it was a most suitable candidate for a haunted house.

The Bull family were somewhat eccentric, in the genteel and harmless way that country clergymen's families were eccentric in those days. The Rev. H.D.E. Bull was an enthusiastic amateur athlete who had enjoyed boxing in his youth and who liked riding to hounds. He would tell of how, after his ordination, he had left the Bishop's palace on a tandem, 'with a tiger up behind'. He would wear clerical dress only on Sundays. He referred to himself as a 'hedge-parson' and to his official duties as 'reading the prayers'. Apart from his somewhat vague ecclesiastical interests and his hunting, he indulged in country pursuits such as lying on the drawing-room floor and potting the rabbits on the lawn with a rook rifle.

The Borley legend was well-established in Bull senior's day. Several of the Bull children claimed to have seen apparitions. Friends who stayed at the Rectory claimed to have seen or heard the coach. Interestingly enough, no spectacular poltergeist effects, for which Borley was later to become famous, were recorded by these witnesses, but only apparitions, auditory effects that were attributed to the death-coach, and furtive noises. There was no hurling of furniture or inexplicable movements of household objects, as there were to be in the high summer of the haunting during the residence at Borley of Marianne and Lionel Foyster.

There was a tradition in the family that the ghost of the nun always appeared on the same day each year, 28 July. One of the Bull daughters recorded a sighting of the nun, and the sighting by four of the daughters on 28 July 1900 has now passed into the Borley canon. Ethel, Frieda and Elsie Bull were returning in the evening from a garden party when they saw a figure in a black robe moving along the Nun's Walk. They called another sister from the house, Dodie, and she also saw the figure. Miss Ethel Bull also claimed to have awoken one night and seen 'an old man in dark, old-fashioned clothes, wearing a tall hat, standing by her bed'.

The provenance and interpretation of these stories has been

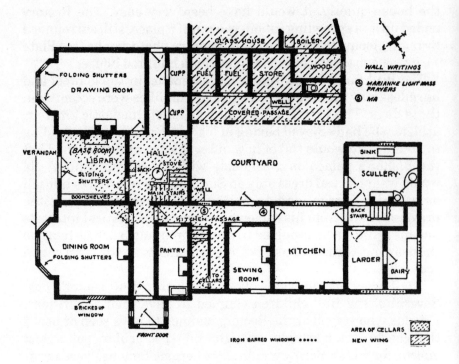

Fig. 1. Borley Rectory: ground floor

exhaustively discussed elsewhere, and here we note only that the tradition of the haunting was well-established long before Marianne came to Borley in 1930 and remind ourselves of the caveat in the introduction cautioning against the confusion between an experience and its interpretation.

After his death in 1892, the Rev. Henry was succeeded by his son the Rev. Harry, who had followed the family tradition of earning his bread by 'reading prayers'. The Rev. Harry, whose full name was Henry Foyster Bull (he was known as 'Harry' to avoid confusion between him and his father), was born in 1863 and educated at Exeter College, Oxford. He remained a bachelor until he was forty-eight and his late marriage and his maiden sisters' hatred of his young bride were woven into the legend of the haunting.

Harry was an odd man, who was subject to fits of somnolence

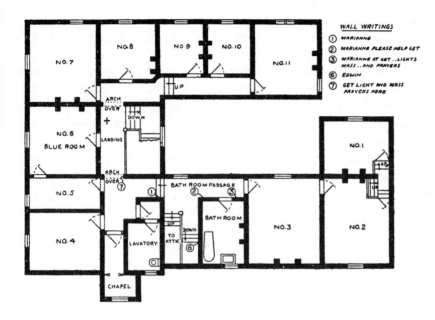

Fig. 2. Borley Rectory: first floor

during which he would vanish for hours at a time as he lay asleep in the extensive Rectory grounds. On one occasion he is said to have burst into tears of vexation because his car wouldn't start. He was very interested in spirits and the after-life and threatened his family with visits from beyond the grave. He kept a large number of cats – almost thirty – which used to follow him when he went out for walks.

Old Harry was convinced that a nun really did haunt his garden, and he not only talked about her in what seemed to be casual and irreverent terms but also indulged in nocturnal vigils in the two summer houses for the express purpose of observing her. His threat to return from beyond the grave is of great significance, given what happened at Borley after his death. Old Harry apparently threatened to produce poltergeist effects from the beyond, though whether to persecute his successors or by way of greeting is not clear. He suggested that his spirit would throw mothballs around to let everyone know he was there; and in the great days of the Borley haunt airborne mothballs were indeed a great hazard.

The Borley cultists make much of the Rev. Harry's belief in the nun. They are, however, overcome with uncharacteristic reticence when they consider Harry's marriage to a widow named Mrs Ivy Brackenbury, and the reaction of his sisters. This is becuse a family feud developed which provides non-supernatural explanations for some of the events at the Rectory after Harry's death.

Ivy Brackenbury kept a sweetshop in Sudbury. She and Harry were married at St Alban's Church, Holborn, on 12 September 1911. Harry was forty-eight and the bride twenty-nine. Harry's maiden sisters bitterly opposed the marriage, which may explain why it was solemnised not at Borley but at an unfashionable London church, and why Mrs Brackenbury took the trouble of living for a while in a nearby women's hostel to obtain the necessary parochial residence.

The sisters not only disliked the bride but also suspected her good faith in marrying a relatively wealthy man who was so much older than she. She probably represented a threat to their own positions, not only because she now became *the* Mrs Bull of Borley, but also because there might be a further division of the family property: at twenty-nine she was well within the upper limit of a woman's child-bearing years.

There is no doubt that some of the Misses Bull ran a campaign of slander and vilification against their new sister-in-law. Various rumours were put about, such as that she wasn't a widow at all but had been abandoned by her former husband 'at the church door', that she hadn't been divorced from this man and her marriage to Harry Bull was therefore bigamous. It seems justice on the Misses Bull that, after putting about such malicious stories, they should invite their cousin Lionel Algernon Foyster and his wife Marianne to take the living of Borley.

After Harry's death at Borley – in the spookily named 'Blue Room' – from chronic bronchitis on 9 June 1927, the sisters continued their campaign. Now the rumours suggested that there was something suspicious about Harry's death. This had profound implications for the course of the alleged haunting. The idea that Harry had suffered an untimely death, coupled with his threats to return, no doubt encouraged people to believe that he too would haunt the Rectory. And sure enough, as we shall soon see, apparitions of Harry Bull *were* seen at Borley. The following quote, taken from a letter to Mrs Guy Smith, the wife of the next incumbent, from a Miss Bull gives some idea of the vigour with which the dear maiden ladies expressed themselves. Referring to her sister in law, Miss Bull wrote: '... that vile woman gets off free and lives to enjoy herself.' For a maiden lady and Rector's daughter to refer to her sister-in-law in such terms suggests that she hated her guts.

After Harry Bull's death Borley was left without a Rector for over a year. Then, on 20 October, 1928, the Rev. Guy Eric Smith, an Anglo-Indian originally from Calcutta, was inducted to the living. Smith and his wife Mabel did not inspect the Rectory before their arrival in the parish and found it dilapidated and far too large – they had no children. They were able to furnish and use only a few rooms and left the rest of the house shut up and empty. There was neither electricity nor running water.

The new Rector and his wife were regaled with ghost stories, both by their parishioners and by the surviving members of the Bull family, who now lived at Cornard near Sudbury. The nun legend was passed on. So were the stories about the Rev. Harry's villainous widow and the mysterious circumstances of his death – the latter having no basis outside his sisters' lively imaginations. It is impossible to tell from the surviving correspondence what the Smiths really made of all this, and whether they really believed that their new and inhospitable home was haunted; their early correspondence with Harry Price and Sydney Glanville, an amateur investigator who became interested in the Borley haunting, suggests that they did; later letters, written long after they had left Borley, suggest that they didn't.

That the Smiths were troubled by the persistent rumours is beyond doubt. Whether or not the Smiths experienced anything during their brief residence that they really believed was of supernatural origin is a matter of conjecture. The evidence, in the form of letters and statements made to psychical researchers over a period of fifteen years, is inconsistent; the Smiths contradicted themselves.

The most extravagant claims were made by their maid, Mary Pearson, who said that she had seen the famous death-coach standing on the Rectory lawn in broad daylight. The experiences of the Smiths themselves are limited to seeing a few shadowy figures leaning over the gates, mysterious dragging footsteps upstairs, lights in the window of an empty room and, on one occasion only, strange whisperings heard by the Rector as he walked along an upstairs passage. Whether or not this rather unimpressive catalogue defies rational explanation, the Smiths' response certainly does; for in June 1929 they wrote to the editor of the *Daily Mirror*, asking him to recommend a psychical research society to deal with their problem.

The next thing that happened to the Rector and his wife was the appearance, not of a phantom nun or a spectral coach on the lawn, but of something far worse: an all too substantial reporter, Mr V.C. Wall of the *Daily Mirror*. In his wake, on 12 June 1929, came the famous Harry Price, whom the *Mirror*'s editor had invited to join in the fun. Borley was about to be transformed from the site of an unremarkable local legend into 'The Most Haunted House in England'.

Other writers on the Borley mystery have concentrated on whether or not the Smiths really did experience anything that could reasonably be described as supernatural. Even the highly sceptical report commissioned by the London Society for Psychical Research does not discuss why the Smiths should have taken this extraordinary – and, as it turned out, disastrous – step of writing to the editor of a national daily paper. None of the explanations given for this make sense. The Borley enthusiasts like to imply – somewhat contrary to the Smiths' own account of their actions – that they were so perturbed by the rumours, *and* by their own and their maid's experiences, that they wished a thorough investigation to be performed by competent authorities. According to this account they applied to the *Daily Mirror* because they did not know of such a competent authority. Now even the most unsophisticated and unworldly clergyman would have had some idea of what was going to happen if he approached the editor of a tabloid newspaper with such a tale; he would not get advice, he would get a reporter and plenty of publicity.

The authors of the report of the Society for Psychical Research let the Smiths off by explaining that it was not they who were upset by the rumours about the Rectory, but their parishioners. This caused the Smiths no little inconvenience because it was difficult to use the Rectory for parish meetings and other social gatherings. While this is plausible, to suggest that the Smiths' response to this would be to contact the *Daily Mirror* with what was, in effect, a newsworthy ghost story is not.

Smith was an ordained and beneficed clergyman of the Church of England. If he had really believed that his Rectory was infested with ghosts, he would have appealed to his Bishop or Archdeacon, not to the editor of the *Daily Mirror*. Surely the spiritual might of the Bishop was what would have brought back the cowering rustics to the Rectory for tea, cake, prayers and discussions about organ lofts and belfries; the temporal might of Fleet Street seems a very poor substitute.

The solution of this problem is given by Mrs Smith's correspondence with Harry Price some years after they had left Borley, when her husband was a clergyman at Sheringham on the Norfolk coast. Mrs Smith wrote of how she was writing a thriller called *Murder at the Parsonage*. She was soliciting Price for advice, and obviously hoping that he would help her to place her manuscript with a publisher.

The title is very significant. Mrs Smith had been regaled with horror stories about the death of Harry Bull. She had also been fed a solid diet of ghost stories which involved tragedy and murder. The Borley haunting was to be plagued with tales of the crimes allegedly committed during the Bull years, ranging from the murder of a kitchen maid who was supposed to have been impregnated by Harry Bull's father, to the poisoning not only of Harry but also of his father. These stories had no factual basis and had their origins in village gossip, slander and the overheated imaginations of various ghost hunters.

The Smiths must have *wanted* publicity. They *wanted* to attract a reporter to Borley and watch him at work. What Mrs Smith was after was material for her supernatural thriller, which was based not only on the traditional legends, but also upon stories invented by the cruel and malicious Bull sisters. Any publicity they received as the residents of a haunted house would of course be of great value when she tried to place her manuscript. Smith's successor, the Rev. Lionel Algernon Foyster (Marianne's husband), did exactly the same; he completed a manuscript, a copy of which is in my possession, entitled *Fifteen Months in a Haunted House*. Foyster's book was a story about a clergyman and his wife and the vicissitudes of their life in a haunted rectory that is recognisable as Borley.

The theory that the Smiths wanted to attract publicity explains their strange and ambiguous attitude to Borley in later years. They were happy to cooperate with Harry Price (of whom more shortly), but when things came to the pass of sworn statements for serious and hard-headed investigators from the Society for Psychical Research, they backed off – much to the disgust of Borley enthusiasts. Mrs Smith felt strongly enough about the matter by 1945 to write the following letter to the *Church Times*.

> Sir, I have read with interest your articles and letters on 'Thump Ghosts', and as I was in residence for some time at Borley Rectory, Sussex [*sic*] ('the most haunted house in England'), I would like to state definitely that neither my husband nor myself believed the house haunted by anything else but rats and local superstition. We left the rectory because of its broken-down condition, but certainly found nothing to fear there.
>
> G. Eric-Smith [*sic*]

Mrs Smith's changes of mind so exasperated the enthusiasts that two of them were moved to write of her: 'Mr Smith died at Sheringham, Norfolk, on 3 August 1940; Mrs Smith continued to live there, her memories confused and unreliable.'

Mrs Smith's later antipathy to Price, with whom she and her husband had cooperated fully earlier, is easily explained. Her literary project was hijacked by Price, just as Foyster's novel was. It was Price, not Foyster or Mrs Smith, who published the bestseller about Borley.

If the Smiths were really after publicity, they were taught a bitter lesson. In approaching the editor of the *Daily Mirror* they animated a Frankenstein's monster that trampled all over the Rectory – literally. The sensational reports carried by the *Mirror* not only made Borley nationally famous overnight, but attracted hordes of rowdy sight-seers, who even invaded the Rectory garden and had to be ejected by the police. The *Daily Mirror* carried Borley reports, written by Wall, on 10, 11, 12, 14, 15 and 17 June 1929. At night car headlights could be seen for miles around converging on the tiny hamlet, bringing spectators who hoped to catch a glimpse of the nun and the death-coach. The Smiths had a dreadful time; and to make it all even worse, Harry Price, the internationally famous psychical investigator, arrived and infested their Rectory with poltergeists.

2

Harry and the Poltergeists

Harry Price became famous as a popular scientific authority on the paranormal and the occult, and as a self-styled 'psychic investigator', in the two decades between the World Wars. During the Thirties no BBC radio broadcast about the paranormal and the occult, and no newspaper feature article speculating on 'survival' or the after-life, was complete without Price's contributions.

Price's life and work reveal a dichotomy between his genuine and, at times, almost passionate desire to investigate thoroughly and scientifically alleged paranormal events (which in the idiom of his times meant the supposed materialisation of spirits by mediums during seances, haunting, poltergeists and telepathy), and his insatiable hunger for publicity and self-advertisement. Eventually he sacrificed the former for the latter and descended to exaggeration, fantasy and blatant fabrication, notably in his sensational accounts of the alleged haunting of Borley.

Price's early life is shrouded in uncertainty because he himself took great pains to conceal it. According to his biographer, Trevor Hall, Price was born into a relatively poor family in Red Lion Square in London. His father was a former grocer who had seduced an under-age girl, Price's mother, and was forced, by the ill-feeling engendered by his delinquency, to give up his shop and become a commercial traveller. This unhappy background seems to have haunted Price for the rest of his life. He later affected not only to be something of a dashing gentleman about town but also to originate from solid country stock in Shropshire, where, he claimed, his father was a wealthy paper manufacturer.

After his secondary education, Price became a travelling salesman himself. His early ambition to become an engineer was frustrated although he attended night-classes in electrical and mechanical engineering. These provided him with the technical skills he later required when setting up his laboratory to investigate 'psychical phenomena'. Price was very ambitious and felt that he had some talent as a writer. At an early age he had become interested in conjuring and the occult. Later in life he confessed that his early ambitions had been to see his name entered in *Who's Who*, to write for the *Encyclopaedia Britannica*, to collect the largest library in the world dedicated to magic and the occult and to be offered an honorary degree by a reputable academic institution for his work on paranormal phenomena. Price achieved all but the last; although he assiduously cultivated men such as Julian Huxley, he never achieved the recognition from the academic world and scientific orthodoxy that he believed he deserved. This was largely his own fault. His lack of restraint when the opportunity for sensational self-publicity presented itself repelled respectable academics and made them deeply suspicious of him and his work. Price, for his part, seems to have interpreted this rejection as social snobbery. His affectations became more peculiar, and he took to adorning his stationery and invitation cards with bogus heraldic devices.

Price was born in 1881. His career before the First World War is unremarkable. He married in 1908, and his wife, a somewhat shadowy figure, was possessed of a sizeable fortune which her husband was later to devote to his various research projects. His interest in conjuring and the occult (he was himself an accomplished amateur conjurer) developed and he began to collect his library. He also began to toy with the idea of using his engineering skills to investigate the alleged miracles performed on the London stage by Vaudeville mediums.

A heart complaint rendered him unfit for active service during the First World War and he worked as the manager of a munitions plant. After the war there was an explosion of interest in Spiritualism, seances and the question of 'survival' because so many families had lost sons, brothers and fathers in the trenches. A crop of bogus mediums sprang up in response to the demand, and Price set himself the task of examining their claims and, if possible, exposing them. In 1920 he joined the Society for Psychical Research. This farcical organisation appears to have expended its energy in violent internal quarrels. The Society boasted many well-known and influential members, notably Sir Arthur Conan Doyle (whose expressions of belief in the most ridiculous alleged spiritualist happenings were becoming increasingly outrageous – he even believed in fairies, literally at the bottom of someone else's garden) and Sir Oliver Lodge, the great physicist, who believed that he had made contact, via a number of mediums, with his son Raymond who had died in the Great War. Price made the acquaintance of such luminaries and began to plan his own organisation dedicated to the scientific study of alleged paranormal events.

Price began his own experiments and made some sensational exposures. He caught out the notorious Hope, who claimed to photograph spirits, and his work stimulated the dramatic though inconclusive *Scientific American* investigation into mediums. In 1923, however, Price discovered the young and pretty 'Stella C' whose supernatural powers were, he asserted, genuine. Price invited Julian Huxley to some of the seances. E.N. Andrade and R.J. Tillyard also came to witness the wonders of 'Stella C'. These authoritative figures confessed that they had been impressed by what they saw. Price was by now fairly launched into the twilight world of psychical investigation and could command attention from both the press and the young British Broadcasting Company.

In 1926, the year before Harry Bull died in the 'Blue Room' at Borley, the doors of Price's National Laboratory for Psychical Research opened in London. Price financed this venture himself. By the standards of the time the laboratory was well-equipped, for Price had provided the latest X-ray, infra-red and photographic apparatus. As well as running his laboratory Price was also Foreign Research officer for the American Society for

Psychical Research, and his statements on the occult and the world to come commanded a wide audience on both sides of the Atlantic.

Price founded his own journals, the presentation and style of which were clearly modelled on the *Proceedings* of the Royal Society of London. The first of his journals was the grandly titled *Proceedings of the National Laboratory of Psychical Research*, which was followed by the *British Journal of Psychical Research* and, from 1931, by the *Bulletin of the National Laboratory for Psychical Research*. None of these lasted beyond a few issues, perhaps because Price himself was the main contributor of articles. None the less Price's fame grew, and he attempted to penetrate academic orthodoxy not only by courting men such as Huxley but also by trying to persuade the University of London to set up a department of psychical research. Somewhat surprisingly this project came close to success.

There is no doubt that many of Price's experiments were carefully and ingeniously contrived. Unfortunately he failed to understand that orthodox science has rigorous and exacting standards and that his work necessarily failed to meet them. The uncertainty and lack of reproducibility of what were supposed to be positive results and the complete absence of any theory of the paranormal phenomena that would allow predictions to be made and tested consigned his work to the fringes of science. Furthermore he showed no restraint in cultivating the popular press and presented his investigations to the public in as sensational a manner as possible. This undoubtedly contributed to the absurd Vaudeville atmosphere that surrounded the National Laboratory.

Among Price's many adventures was the exposure of Mrs Helen Duncan, the materialising medium. He demonstrated that she was able, by virtue of an anatomical abnormality, to swallow rubber gloves, safety pins, yards of cheesecloth and other apparatus which she would later regurgitate in the privacy of her magical cabinet and fashion into somewhat unconvincing 'spirit figures' in the semi-darkness of the seance room. But the ambition of every psychical researcher is not to expose frauds but to find something genuine. The trouble is that in the end all they have to show for their pains *is* shabby frauds. Unless they are interested in the psychopathology of their subjects they reach dead-ends.

Price undoubtedly became frustrated with his work. That he threw over careful experimentation for sensational public announcements and column inches is shown by two of his investigations: the 'haunting' of Cashens Gap in the Isle of Man by an oracular mongoose named 'Gef', which was said to sing 'Home on the range' from the top of a wardrobe when light-hearted and 'Jesus my Saviour on Calvary's Tree' from the same eminence when maudlin; and his adventures in the Hartz mountains with 'Professor' Joad, when the two men attempted (unsuccessfully) to transform a goat into a 'fair youth' with the aid of a magic spell. Price is alleged to have said of the general public, 'They don't want the *debunk*, they want *the bunk*, and that is what I'll give them.' The indications are that he carried out his threat.

*

Price arrived at Borley as the very model of a modern psychical researcher, complete with a list of equipment that included 'soft felt overshoes for creeping about', 'a supply of flashbulbs', 'a hank of electrical flex', 'a flask of brandy in case the investigator or his assistant are taken ill', and his assistant herself, the glamorous Miss Lucie Kaye.

Borley was, of course, already in an uproar. Coach trips were even being organised to bring sight-seers from neighbouring towns. Price threw himself into this charade with gusto, and it has often been remarked that as soon as he appeared on the scene the haunting took on a quite different character. Violent poltergeist activity broke out, which had not hitherto been a significant feature of the supernatural wonders. What now began to happen was of a quite different order from servant girls telling the gentlemen down from London that they'd seen a funny old coach and a pair of bay horses on the lawn. According to Price's own account:

We descended the main staircase and had just reached the hall when another crash was heard and we found that a glass candlestick, one of a pair that we'd just seen on the mantelpiece of the Blue Room, had been hurled down the main stairs, had struck the iron stove, and had finally distintegrated in a thousand fragments on the floor. Both Mr Wall and I saw the candlestick hurtle past our heads. We at once dashed upstairs, made another search, and found nothing. We returned to the hall. We turned out all the lights, and the entire party sat in complete darkness, just waiting. A few minutes later we heard something come rattling down the stairs and Mr Wall said he had been hit on the hand. We then relighted the lamps and found it was a mothball which, apparently, had followed the same path as the candlestick.

In quick succession, and in full light, the following articles came tumbling down the stairs: first of all, sea shore pebbles; then a piece of slate, then some more pebbles.

Now Harry Bull is said to have threatened to haunt the Rectory by throwing moth-balls about. The plot thickens when we read more of Price's account of the seance that was later held upstairs on the same night as the throwing of the moth-ball – or rather, early on the morning of the next day. Taking part were Price, Miss Lucie Kaye, Mr V.C. Wall of the *Daily Mirror*, the Rector and his wife, *and two of the Misses Bull*, the late Harry Bull's sisters.

In order to open the proceedings, I said … 'If any entity is present here tonight, will it please make its presence known?' … Just as we were wondering whether we were wasting our time, a faint – though sharp and decisive – tap was heard coming from, apparently, the window …

The participants in the seance located the site of the rapping at the back of a dressing-table mirror. They tried to talk to the 'entity' using the time-honoured code of one tap for 'yes', two for 'don't know' and three for 'yes'. It all sounds like a game-show, which in a sense it was. Readers unfamiliar with seances of this kind should understand clearly that the 'entity' can volunteer nothing – it can only respond to the leading questions put by the sitters. The only other method of communication is via a numerical scheme of spelling out the letters of the alphabet – the number of taps corresponding to the letters of the alphabet in their normal order. This is clearly very laborious, and would render an illiterate 'entity' all but inarticulate.

And sure enough the rapping 'entity' identified himself as Harry Bull. According to Price, there was a brief exchange about whether it was Harry's footsteps people had heard in the house, and whether he was happy, and then the Misses Bull were invited to question their brother's shade about family affairs.

> At this juncture I asked the Misses Bull and Mr and Mrs Smith whether they would like to question the entity – the alleged Harry Bull – as to certain private affairs of the family. They said they would and for about an hour a string of questions was put to the entity ... great difficulty was experienced in obtaining names or messages by spelling out the alphabet ... whatever it was 'tapping', did not appear to grasp the technique of this method of communication. Obviously the questions asked by the Misses Bull cannot be printed here.

Mr Wall wrote an account of this episode that appeared in the *Daily Mirror* on 15 June 1929 under the headline: *Seance held in Haunted House. Mysterious Rappings in the Rectory of Borley. 'Former Rector'. How questions were asked and answered.* This agrees with Price's although the tone is rather facetious. Of the questioning of Harry Bull by his sisters, Wall wrote:

> Here followed a series of questions dealing with the late Mr Bull's private affairs, to which no answer at all was received.

SEANCE HELD IN
HAUNTED HOUSE

Mysterious Rappings in the
Rectory of Borley

"FORMER RECTOR"

How Questions Were Asked and
Answered

A partial record of this question and answer session has been
preserved in the notes compiled by Sydney H. Glanville. He
became interested in the Borley haunting some years later, and
interviewed the Smiths on 6 October 1937, when they were
living in Sevington in Kent. They gave him the following
account:

During a seance held at the Rectory, in Mr and Mrs Smith's
bedroom, taps were heard coming from the back of Mrs
Smith's mirror, these taps had been heard by her for some
weeks before. Mr Harry Price who had arranged the seance,
asked Mr and Mrs Smith if they would join the 'circle', and
invited them to ask questions, the following were among
the questions asked:
  Is that Harry Bull?
  Yes. (three taps)
  Are you happy?
  No. (two taps)
  Do you mind Mr and Mrs Smith being here?
  No.
  Is there money trouble?
  Yes.
  Were you killed?
  Yes.
Mr and Mrs Smith were so upset that they asked that the
seance be stopped at once. This was done immediately, and
they refused to allow any further sittings in the house.

No doubt the Misses Bull, who, the reader will remember, were present at the seance, asked these questions. They were slandering their sister-in-law again and literally putting words into their dead brother's mouth. The cantankerous old spinsters felt that they had been cheated out of their inheritance by Harry Bull's widow. Mrs Smith's literary aspirations, and perhaps her sense of romance, led her to embrace their stories and to add her own fuel to the fire. Glanville's notes contain the following information, which is based on his interview with the Smiths:

> Henry (Harry) Foyster Bull, son of the late Rev. H.D.E. Bull was Rector of B——— from 1892 to 1927. He died in Bedroom (No. 7) [*sic*]. He married a Mrs——— of S———, who formerly had a small sweetshop there. She was a married woman, whose husband is still living and, so far as is known, still is. There had been no divorce. By his will he left her a life interest in his estate, instead of to his sisters. He was found dead, and no one was present at the time of death. His wife nursed him exclusively during his last illness.

In another passage we learn that:

> During the first few weeks, before they moved into the Rectory, Mrs Smith found that one of the cellar doors was locked, the farther one and, on enquiring from the gardener, learnt that it had never been opened 'to his knowledge'. However, by the time they actually moved in, it had been opened by someone. Mrs Smith found it piled with empty wine bottles. Upon turning some of these over, she came on a small bottle labelled 'Poison'. It appeared to be more recent than the other bottles, cleaner.

Glanville might as well have accused Bull's widow outright. This totally fictitious story of Harry Bull's murder was to plague Borley for years, and no doubt caused his widow great distress. The whole farrago was based on nothing more than village gossip and the malice of the Misses Bull, who, one feels, were lucky not to have ended up in a court of law. They were not only insulting Ivy Bull, but also accusing her of a serious crime – murder.

That the Misses Bull were prepared to fantasise and lie about their brother's death leads to the suspicion that they were prepared to do the same about the ghostly nun.

Glanville interviewed them on 25 June 1938 and made the following notes:

These two sisters live with a third, and a brother, Mr Gerald Bull at Chilton Lodge, Great Cornard, Sudbury, Suffolk. They are the children of the late Rev. Henry Dawson Ellis Bull. The Rev. Harry Bull was a brother.

The Rev. H.D.E. Bull built the existing Rectory and, as his family grew, added the new wing. He had fourteen children, twelve of whom survived. He was a good boxer. He hunted regularly and from their report appears to have been the typical old-fashioned country parson. Both sisters declare that he had no 'nickname', they definitely say that they never heard of one.

They allege that a Nunnery formerly stood on the site of the present Rectory, or very near. They both stoutly maintain that the Rectory has always been haunted by the Nun, and by other manifestations. They both say that, with their sister, they all clearly saw the Nun walking slowly across the garden on a sunny July afternoon. Her head was bowed and her hands clasped together in front of her, hanging at full length.

They agree that their brother, the late Rev. Harry Bull, walks down the main stairs, enters the library and stands in the room. He carries a small bag or manuscript case and is dressed in his dressing-gown.

Miss Ethel Bull says that for years she frequently heard a knock on her bedroom door, investigation never disclosed any cause for this. Further she says that, on a great many occasions, she was awakened by the presence of the figure of a man in a tall hat, standing beside her bed.

Regarding the life and death of their brother the Rev. Harry Bull

He married, at St Albans, Holborn in 1911, a Mrs Brackenbury (widow) and formerly a nurse at the local hospital (Sudbury). They say that her previous husband (Harold? Brackenbury) left her at the door of the church after the marriage. That she had a daughter by this marriage. Their brother's married life was very unhappy. They allege that their brother died from the effects of poison and that, after his death, they found a bottle half-filled with 'sugar of lead' in the cellar.

Their brother often mentioned to them that he intended altering his will, by which he had left his wife a life interest in his estate.

Thus not only Mrs Smith found poison in the cellar, but also the Misses Bull; that the Misses Bull were malicious old crones who had put about a libellous story concerning their sister-in-law is without doubt. Mrs Smith took it up for her own reasons – her literary project; and as we shall see, Marianne adapted it to her own requirements when she too wanted to see a ghost.

The activities of the Misses Bull are important because 'Harry Bull' repeatedly communicated with sitters at seances when the Borley mystery was 'investigated' by amateur spiritualists such as Mr Glanville. The murder of Harry Bull became part of the Borley canon. Trevor Hall thoroughly investigated the circumstances of Harry Bull's death and the claims that his marriage was bigamous, and found that the Misses Bull's story was false. Harry's death certificate was in order, and his marriage had not been bigamous.

*

We have already seen that the Borley haunting became quite different when Harry Price appeared on the scene, because violent poltergeist activity, which had not hitherto been a significant feature of the ghostly practices, broke out on a wild scale. Price has been accused of fraud and trickery at Borley. He was, after all, a skilled amateur conjurer. After Price's death in 1948 a reporter for the *Daily Mail* even claimed that during a visit to Borley he had caught the great investigator red-handed with his pockets full of pebbles. Lord Charles Hope, a distinguished member of the Society for Psychical Research, whom Price also took to Borley, expressed the opinion that the poltergeist effects had a natural, and not a supernatural, origin.

That Price was caught out at Borley – the *Daily Mail* reporter claimed that he had not revealed this incident until after Price's death because the only other witness was Price's own secretary, and that printing an account would have precipitated a libel action against him – is born out by Price's curious attitude to the allegedly haunted Rectory. Poltergeist activity of the violence, and on the scale, reported by Price at Borley would surely have been irresistible to a committed investigator of such matters, whatever other pressing projects he was engaged upon. Borley presented a rare opportunity for a careful scientific study. Yet after late 1929, he did not go near the place and contented himself with a desultory correspondence with the Smiths, who had in any case moved out on 14 July 1929 and gone to live in nearby Long Melford. From there they ran the parish until April 1930, when they moved to Sheringham in Norfolk.

When Price finally returned to Borley on 13 October 1931, he would not meet Mrs Smith as his hostess, but Marianne Emily Rebecca Foyster. And Marianne had already met the shade of the late Rev. Harry Foyster Bull.

3

Going Bump in the Night

In September 1931, Harry Price received a visit at his London laboratory from two of the Misses Bull, who informed him that the most remarkable things were happening at the Rectory. Household objects were moving of their own volition or disappearing into thin air only to appear somewhere else, the new Rector's wife – Marianne – had seen apparitions of the late Harry Bull, mysterious messages were scribbled on the walls, and more than once, the Rector's wife had been hurled out of bed by unseen forces. The Rev. Lionel Algernon Foyster, their cousin through their mother, and Marianne, his wife, seemed to be in actual physical danger. In Price's own words:

It can be said without fear of contradiction that the Foyster occupation coincided with the noisiest, most violent, and most dangerous period in the whole history of the Borley manifestations.

Since the Misses Bull took the initiative by visiting Price, and since Foyster himself also wrote to him, it is clear that he had made a favourable impression on these ladies during his first visit. If they suspected him of trickery, this did not deter them from involving him again. Foyster was warned by the Society for Psychical Research to beware of Price, but, in spite of this, he allowed him to visit Borley. The letters written to Price by Foyster are worth quoting in full. On 3 October 1931:

Dear Mr Price, Thank you for your letter of 2nd. inst. I am enclosing my accounts of occurrences. I would explain that these were written chiefly to send round to members of my family and therefore no explanation is given to matters in which they were not needed for them, but might be for strangers. I had better state that 'Marianne' is my wife: 'Adelaide' our little girl aged 3½ now, the 'C.L.' is a circular letter that circulated round our family – Harry Bull, as probably you were aware, is my cousin, and 'Ivy' is his wife. Ally Bull is Harry's brother.

My last account takes the story up to June 24. Since then we have been quieter on the whole, but we have had some outbreaks similar to those recorded. One evening in August, I think, I was in the church, when my wife came rushing over and said that there was a tremendous noise emanating from my study and she wanted me to come over and see what it was. We went in together and found that the furniture, etc. had been thrown about and the room was in confusion. One night last week, I was woken up at about 3.30 a.m. by being hit on the head by something which proved to be a large, empty water jug from another bedrom. We put it on the floor (it was not broken) and presently while we were still both awake it was thrown at, or dropped on, my wife.

Our chief trouble lately has been from things disappearing, sometimes from almost under our eyes; these sometimes have been returned later; also from doors being locked. My wife during a recent illness was twice locked in her room; once there was no one in the house and she was locked in from the outside – one key left in the door and the other laid on a chest of drawers close by; the other time I had one key in my pocket by day and under my pillow by night; under my pillow that morning by mistake [*sic*]. It had gone and when we were locked out of our room one night and had to sleep elsewhere, while the little girl was locked in her room, for which we had no key. These opened the next day after a 'relic' had been applied to them.

I should be very much obliged if you would kindly not

mention at Long Melford, what your business down here is, since we do not want reports to get around the parish. We have one indoor servant at present, but I think with care, we can keep her from hearing anything. She is quite young – not 15 yet – has only been here ten days, and has as yet not come up against any 'demonstration'. She has of course heard the gossip of the neighbourhood about the house, but does not, I think, believe it. We should like to keep her as long as possible as she is a help to my wife, who is not well.

Yours faithfully,
(signed) L.A. Foyster

The reader would be justified in concluding that this was not the letter of a well man. Between 3 and 9 October, however, Foyster must have received the warning from the Society for Psychical Research, for he wrote again in a quite different tone on 9 October:

Dear Mr Price, Thank you for your letter of 6th. inst. in which you say we are to expect you next Tuesday evening. I trust you will not mind my asking that all those who are taking any part in the investigation will, before the investigation starts, sign an undertaking that they will neither themselves publish nor cause to be published in any newspaper or periodical in this or any other country, or in any other way make public the facts connected with the case. The condition I have made is in self-defence or we might find our position here impossible and land ourselves in serious difficulties.

I intended to say in a previous letter that I should like to have my MS of the occurrences [*word illegible*] back, when you have finished with them.

Yours faithfully,
(signed) L.A. Foyster

Price, this time in the company of Mrs K.M. Goldney, the Secretary of the Society for Psychical Research, duly visited Borley on 13 and 14 October 1931. His published description of the visit is as follows:

> We had a long chat with Mr Foyster, and heard a good deal
> of what had been happening there. It was an amazing story
> ... We found Mr Foyster a delightful, typical cultured
> parson of the best type, a scholar, a Cambridge (Pembroke)
> M.A., and much travelled. His wife, Marianne, was younger
> than he, bright vivacious, and intelligent. It seemed strange
> that they should have been the focus of such unpleasant
> incidents as had occurred at the Rectory.

Plate 3 shows Marianne in 1922. Plate 4 shows Foyster,
Marianne, Harry Price and Mrs Goldney standing in front of the
Rectory. The reader will, after reading the following chapters, be
able to judge whether Foyster could reasonably be described as
'a typical cultured parson of the best sort'. But what of the
'unpleasant incidents' that had occurred at the Rectory?

The supposed supernatural events witnessed by the Foysters,
which made their lives miserable, are of a different order from
the tittle-tattle and dubious memories of the Misses Bull.
Although Foyster had visited the Rectory in his youth and knew
about the legend of the nun, he and Marianne had recently
returned from Canada to take up the living and had been away
from Borley for many years. The poltergeist activity observed
during the Smiths' residence can be explained as tricks played
by naughty Harry Price, who was carrying into execution his
threat to give them the bunk. But Price never visited Borley
during the violent and extraordinary period from October 1930,
when the Foysters arrived, to the summer of 1931. The Foysters'
stories cannot be dismissed lightly.

Foyster has left three written accounts of his experiences at
Borley; these are his *Summary of Experiences at Borley Rectory*,
written in early 1938 (after he had retired) as a digest for Harry
Price; his *Diary of Occurrences at Borley Rectory*, written in 1931
before Price's visit; and *Fifteen Months in a Haunted House*,
which was written as a novel with thinly disguised characters
and locations, which Foyster had serious hopes of publishing. He
worked on this for many years.

It is worth quoting Foyster's *Summary of Experiences* in full. The reader will, I hope, realise that, although Foyster was undoubtedly an eccentric, who was prepared to attribute supernatural origins to workaday domestic incidents, something out of the ordinary was happening at the Rectory. Price was correct when he described what was going on as 'an amazing story'.

SUMMARY OF EXPERIENCES AT BORLEY RECTORY

October 16 1930. My wife (referred to as M.F.), little girl aged 2 yrs, 7 months (referred to as A.), and myself came into residence.

First experiences of anything out of the ordinary. A voice heard calling M.F.'s name. Harry Bull seen at different times by M.F. between study and bedroom above. Jugs and other utensils disappearing and coming back. Peculiar smells – especially one most nearly resembling lavender – noticeable particularly in our bedroom. Bells rung; a bracelet is detached from wrist-watch while M.F. is in room only a few feet away and no one else besides A., who was in her room, is in the house. Bracelet was taken away and has never been seen since. Lavender bag, which no one has seen before, discovered on M.F.'s sewing-room mantelpiece. Disappears and appears again in my pocket: discovered when putting on coat one morning.

1931
February. Books found on windowsill of w.c. As soon as one is taken away, replaced by another. (These books had been left by the Bulls and stowed away on shelf in house-maid's pantry.) Last of these – torn cover thrown on floor.

25th. A big return of crockery. M.F. asks for a teapot; this is also returned. At my suggestion asks for bracelet, but in very uncomplimentary language.

26th. Books found under our bed in the morning. A consignment of hymn books, unknown of before, discovered in the rack over the kitchen range in the afternoon. In the evening M.F. is given a terrific blow in the eye – a cut under

it, black eye next day – by an invisible assailant on the
landing just outside bedroom; she is carrying a candle.

27th. Shortly after we have retired and the light is
extinguished, first, a cotton reel, then a hammer-head with
a broken handle attached is thrown across our bed. Lamp
lit and throwing discontinued.

28th. I write a letter on the subject. Directly afterwards
(the room had been empty for a few minutes in between)
two pins with their points sticking upwards, one on seat of
armchair, other on chair I had been sitting on. About an
hour or so later an erection composed of an old lamp and
saucepan (neither of them seen before) found outside my
door. Later a floor-polisher handle is put across the passage
I traversed on my way to supper, and later again a tin of
bath salts placed just inside bathroom door trips up M.F.

March 5th. Two articles thrown after lights were out in
our bedroom; then, after an interval, I was aroused by a
hairbrush on my head.

March 6th. The knob off a door thrown with some force
from just behind M.F. as she comes along the bathroom
passage.

March 7th. M.F. thrown at in the afternoon. In the evening
I attempt to exorcise spirits; stone hits me on shoulder.
Books thrown out of shelves in M.F.'s sewing-room.
Pictures in hall and on staircase taken down and laid on
ground. Things thrown in bedroom. (This night window was
closed.)

March 8th. At night, after carefully looking under bed,
both doors in bedroom locked, more throwing. (First
window open few inches at bottom, then at top. Verandah
outside would make throwing in very difficult.)

March 9th. (Monday) Although plumber's men in the
house thawing out pipes, stones roll down back stairs and
odd things found in kitchen passage. A visitor in the
afternoon inspects the attics and is satisfied no one could be
hiding there, hears a bell ring, and sees a stone almost as it
came to rest which we heard descending the back stairs.
M.F. enters house just afterwards. Evidence it was not she.

Many incidents that afternoon and evening, amongst them
M.F. hearing noise outside sewing room door (shut) at
about three yards distance from it, a stone from behind
touches her hair. Later coming again from kitchen sees
piece of iron coming after her (but not the being carrying it);
it is thrown in behind her just inside sewing-room door as
she hastily dashes in and pulls door to. In kitchen as M.F. is
making up fire, a stone flies out and hits further door as I go
behind it. Two duplex lamps in room at time.

March 10th. A little pile of five stones found behind
M.F.'s pillow when she woke in the morning. More objects
carried into the house. A stone through a pane in staircase
window thrown from inside while M.F., A. and myself are
standing by hall stove. I think this night a small tin
travelling trunk (not seen before) suddenly noticed in
kitchen while we are sitting at supper there. This stayed in
the house for some days, but eventually disappeared. China
powder box and wedding ring discovered in bathroom: later
disappeared during the following morning. M.F. stumbles
over brick placed outside bathroom door. Next morning two
stones found behind my pillow.

March 11th. Two Anglican priests go thoroughly over
house with M.F. and self using incense, holy water and
prayers. Presence of sort felt, but no active demonstration.
Later a stone thrown at boy from cottage. I was out most of
the remaining part of the day. After my return, stone
thrown at me; then as we three are standing round the hall
stove, another stone fell only a few inches from my head.

March 12th. Clean linen taken out of the kitchen
cupboard and trailed over the floor.

March 13th. M.F. hit on the head and hurt by a piece of
metal thrown down back stairs. A piece of brick dropped on
supper table close by my plate, but without breaking or
touching any crockery.

March 15th. As I am typing out a diary of events in the
house, first my collar, which I had taken off for comfort, is
thrown at me, then a stick and a piece of coke are thrown
across the room.

March 16th. M.F. in early morning finds kitchen table upside down and contents of store cupboard partly inside and partly scattered broadcast. In the evening, bedroom window which had been left open, discovered closed the wrong way round.

March 23rd. M.F. carrying a tray in one hand and a lamp in the other up the front stairs, has the inside of an iron thrown at her from a few feet ahead. It breaks the lamp chimney.

March 24th. Small articles thrown at M.F. sweeping, etc. outside bedroom. Harry Bull seen again by M.F. about this time and (probably) by cottage tenant, through stair window at night.

March 28th. M.F. sees a monstrosity (seen by her and others on other occasions) near kitchen door. It touches her shoulder with iron-like touch.

March 29th. Palm Sunday. Still.

April 11th. Saturday in Easter week, when there was a small demonstration. Absolute quiet, with this one exception, during Holy Week and Easter Week.

April. Milk jug is mysteriously found empty. I request a clean one and make a rude remark about drinking after the ghosts. While we are sitting at tea in broad daylight with doors and windows closed, missiles are thrown at me. At night I count up to 12 or 13 times I was thrown at between approximately 6 p.m. and 11 p.m. in different parts of the house.

May. A bad half-hour in the kitchen one evening ended by my going upstairs to get creosote with which we fumigate the house. On my way up a lump of dried mortar hits me in the neck. On the way down a metal spanner goes through my hair. After fumigation the trouble stops at once; pepper, however, dropped on us in bed – some had previously been thrown into M.F.'s face in kitchen. Next evening M.F. does some fumigating but is rather lenient with the creosote. Bells ring, stone thrown at her and jam jar crashes against kitchen door as she is returning. I go round with creosote and trouble ceases.

Next day (Monday) I collect six articles thrown in the late afternoon to shew Sir George and Lady Whitehouse who arrived at about 9 p.m. to see if anything was doing. While they are here, skirting board of unused bedroom (not entered by anyone that day as far as we knew) discovered to be on fire. Some throwing after it had been put out. We accept invitation and stay a few days with Whitehouse. One evening when up at Borley M.F. sees paper in the air; it at once falls to ground: discovered to have some hardly decipherable writing on it. Next day when we come up, it had disappeared. Other pieces of paper with 'Marianne' (M.F.'s name) in childish hand were found from time to time about the house.

June 6. Worst outburst begins with a stone being thrown.

June 7. Stones thrown in the evening. A chair in spare room where M.F. was in bed very unwell, twice thrown over. Strange noises heard on landing during the night: bangs: taps on door, etc.

June 8 (Monday) Soon after 10 a.m. proceedings start. These include a variety of things; books, stones, clothes, suit case, a clothes basket full of soiled linen (twice) thrown over the balustrade from the landing to stairs and hall. M.F. hears turmoil going on in what was usually our bedroom; gets up from sick-bed to see; noise at once stops, but room found to be in confusion; bed moved, furniture overturned; doctor calls and witnesses some throwing; Edwin Whitehouse visits house and also witnesses some throwing. M.F. turned out of bed three times during the day, but each time when alone in the room. Lady Whitehouse coming up in the evening hears more throwing. Matters are so bad that she and Sir George insist on us going down to their house for a time.

During the rest of the month, house empty at night except a few nights that I could get someone else to sleep in the house as well. On one of these, when F. de Arles* was there, hearing a noise just before retiring I went to his room

* We shall soon learn much more about F. de Arles.

to see if it came from there: found him asleep and an empty paint pot, which he said he knew nothing about, placed close up against the door inside. August. A medium and an investigator come down and hold a seance. Different spirits are tackled, amongst them Joe Miles who, it was declared, was responsible for the disturbances. However, it appeared subsequently that this was a mistake.

August or Sept. Study attacked. Writing desk thrown down on its face; chairs overturned; books pushed out of the shelves; room in confusion.

September. We are locked out of our room one night. A. locked into hers. (Doors unlocked with help of relic of Curé d'Ars.)

Sept. 26. On the kitchen being left empty for a few minutes, a saucepan full of potatoes left on the stove found to have been emptied. Witnessed by M.F. and a maid. (N.B. We had no resident maid in the house from the time we arrived till Sept. 1931.)

About this time things were moving about in the house (or disappeared altogether) to a great extent. Amongst them a big pile of typewritten sheets; a small portable typewriter. Money, though moved, we cannot be certain was ever taken.

October. Visit of Mr Harry Price and three members of his council. On the first evening bell rang; bottle crashed on front stairs and other things thrown. M.F., who not being well had gone to bed, had first one then the other door of her room locked. One came unlocked in answer to prayer. Council next day declared their opinion that M.F. was responsible for phenomena. She was put under surveillance, but bell from bedroom rang while she was being surveyed.

I am awakened one morning by having a water jug dropped on my head. I left it on the floor and a little time afterwards it is dropped on M.F.'s head.

Oct-Novem. The report that a shadowy form said by visitor to the house and by former occupants to be seen in the room over the kitchen, is true, has confirmation from A.

Being sent to lie down in that room one afternoon, she came downstairs with a bruise under her eye. On being asked how she got it, she answered: 'A nasty thing by curtain in my room gave it to me.'

This apparition said to be seen also one early morning entering our bedroom. I was up and M.F. still asleep, so neither of us saw it.

November 13. A rather serious demonstration this evening, witnessed also by Edwin Whitehouse and our maid. (I ceased keeping an exact diary of events in June. There were therefore various phenomena in the way of throwing, doors being locked, etc. during these last months that are unrecorded but nothing very different to what we had experienced that I can think of – except one evening just after I came in a pot of, apparently, freshly made tea that no one owned to having made, was placed in the dining room for me. However I could not be quite sure about the history of this.)

January 1932. One night both doors of our room found locked – one from inside; the other communicating with dressing room, had a chest of drawers pulled right up against it inside, showing the impossibility, therefore, of the locking having been done by a human agent. Once more we seek admission by means of prayer. Door still found locked. We go into chapel and while there a terrific noise starts up in the hall, which we find is due to cat with claw stuck in rat trap. When we returned a key is found lying on the corner of the altar, which turns out to be that of door between bedroom and dressing room. January. Offer to come and help us get rid of ghosts from Mr Warren of the Marks Tey spiritualist circle. He and H.H. Frost come over and talk to us.

Jan 23-24. Finally they come with a medium on Jan 23 suggesting spending next night in the house. Directly they come, throwing begins, so I suggest their spending that night instead. Warren and Frost go over to get other members of the circle, leaving medium with us. Great demonstrations – bottles dashing down back stairs; kitchen passage strewn with broken glass, etc.; bells ringing; quieted down from some time, but starts up somewhat when the rest of the circle return. Party stayed till 5 a.m. and then leave with the belief that the trouble has been arrested. Next morning the house entirely different; demonstrations definitely stop (with two exceptions noted below) till 1935.

(I have a copy of the circle's own report of the proceedings. If you would like to have one, the secretary is: H.H. Frost, the Mill House, Layer-de-la-Haye, Colchester, who I think would probably be pleased to furnish any information.)

1932 May. Some members of the Marks Tey circle come over one afternoon. According to what they say were orders 'from the other side', we sit in the study with the room darkened and the gramophone playing. M.F. who was not at all well that day, goes off into deep sleep from which she awakens very much better. Just after this a stone thrown down back stairs while F. de Arles and self are passing along kitchen passage. Attributed to a 'little spare power floating round unused'.

June. One evening two objects are thrown. On writing to inform the circle, they reply that they were told that there might be some trouble in June, but things would be quiet afterwards. They come over on three or four evenings during the month. On one of these while we are sitting in the study, spirit of late well-known psychic researcher is seen by Mr Warren, but by no one else.

1933 June. One evening I hear strange noises in the house I cannot account for, but nothing further follows.

1935. Some indications of a little trouble starting up again. A few things disappear in unaccountable ways.

August. Bank Holiday. M.F., A. and self and friend having tea on study verandah: noises, much like a picture falling heard in drawing room: investigation, however, reveals nothing out of place. These continue at intervals, some upstairs. About 13 or 14 bangs heard altogether.

October. We move out of the house.

Foyster's *Summary of Experiences* is an extraordinary

document. The reader should understand that this was used by Price as source material, and that Foyster's experiences at Borley (and those of his wife, Marianne) form a corner-stone of the whole Borley cult. Although Foyster wrote it in early 1938, after he had retired and was living in the roof of a bungalow in Ipswich under somewhat startling circumstances that will be described in their place, the peculiarities of his account cannot be explained by the onset of senility between 1935 and 1938. The accounts left by Foyster that were written while he was Rector of Borley from 1930 to 1935 are no less bizarre.

While most readers will not, I hope, consider Foyster's writing convincing evidence for the reality of poltergeists, they will be as fascinated as I was when I first read them. What on earth was going on? Why did the Rev. Foyster attribute supernatural causes to the emptying of a milk jug? Who put pins on his chair? Why was he persecuted? What was the mysterious relic of the Curé d'Ars that miraculously opened doors that had been supernaturally locked? Who was F. de Arles who slept at the Rectory and denied all knowledge of the enigmatic paint pot found behind his bedroom door?

It is obvious that the domestic arrangements at Borley Rectory were of an unusual kind, and that behind the ghostly tales lies a much more interesting, and hitherto untold, story. That Borley was a madhouse during the Foysters' residence is confirmed by the other accounts of the haunting in which Foyster elaborates on the brief descriptions given in his *Summary of Experiences*. Extracts from his diary and novel will be given later in this book, and we shall see that Foyster made some significant omissions when he was compiling his *Summary* in 1938.

4

The Most Haunted House in England

The Foysters lived at Borley from October 1930 until October 1935, when Foyster retired because of his failing health. He was, as we shall see, a man sick in both mind and body. The Rectory was left empty, for when a new Rector, the Rev. A.C. Henning, was appointed a united benefice was created from the parishes of Borley and neighbouring Liston. Because of the poor condition of Borley Rectory and its lack of amenities, Henning chose to live at Liston. Borley might have sunk back into the obscurity of local legend if Harry Price had not decided to intervene.

A careful reader of Foyster's *Summary of Experiences* will have noticed a surprising admission by the author: 'Visit by Mr Harry Price and his council ... Council next day expressed their opinion that M.F. was responsible for the phenomena.' This is the more amazing in the light of what Price was later to write in his books, *The Most Haunted House in England* and *The End of Borley Rectory*, which contain no hint that he was sceptical about the supernatural origin of the indoor sports that were causing the Rector so much discomfort.

When Price visited Borley in October 1931 (his only visit to Borley while the Foysters were living there and the poltergeists at their worst), he was sufficiently convinced that Marianne was responsible for the bell-ringing, stone-throwing, locking and unlocking of doors, mobile lavender bags and miraculous draughts of hymn books in the drying rack to confide his opinion to her husband, who was angry at the suggestion; Price left Borley on bad terms with both the Foysters, and he was not to return until 1937, almost two years after they had left. When Price was collecting material for his first Borley book, in which he made good his threat to give the public bunk, he wrote to Foyster and asked him for his first-hand accounts of the wonders witnessed by the Rector and his wife during their residence. Foyster wrote back as follows:

Jan. 7th, 1938
Dear Mr. Price, In reply to yours of the 5th. inst. I was somewhat surprised at its contents, since, when you and some members of your council visited in 1931, the opinion was expressed that it was my wife who was responsible for the phenomena.

Price never believed that Borley was haunted. He was, however, an astute and agreeable old fraudster who saw that there was money to be made if the matter was handled with care. He decided to rent the empty Rectory himself, and his tenancy began on 19 May 1937. Instead of living there himself and conducting his own investigation, he recruited teams of amateur ghost hunters who took turns at staying overnight in the empty, gloomy, deserted house. Price placed an advertisement in *The Times* on 25 May 1937, which read as follows:

Haunted House – responsible persons of leisure and intelligence, intrepid, critical, and unbiassed, are invited to join rota of observers in a year's night and day investigation of alleged haunted house in Home Counties. Printed instructions supplied. Scientific training or ability to operate simple instruments an advantage. House situated in lonely hamlet, so own car is essential. Write to Box H. 989 The Times. E.C.4.

This was a shrewd move. Whatever aspersions might be cast upon his own veracity, Price could appeal to the social and professional status of his observers. He recruited a large number of middle-class men, ranging from Oxbridge undergraduates to Squadron Leaders. Among them was Mr Sydney H. Glanville, whom the reader has already met, and who took such a great interest in Borley that he began his own investigation and compiled *The Locked Book of Borley Rectory*.

Price primed his observers by giving them a printed handbook in which the Borley legend and the alleged experiences of previous occupants of the house were set out in some detail. In other words he was suggesting what they should see during their lonely vigils. No doubt Price was relying on the powers of suggestion; it is not unreasonable to suppose that even intrepid, critical and unbiassed men of leisure and intelligence who have been told ghost stories and then left to spend the night in the very house that is supposed to be haunted would deliver the desired goods.

Perhaps Price underestimated his men; for their collection of 'Observers' Reports', another cornerstone of the Borley cult, is disappointing. The most spectacular effects (or 'demonstrations', as the Rev. Foyster would have called them) were a luminous patch on a ceiling and the mysterious movement of a bag of coal. The value of the experiment, and the significance of the evidence, has been exhaustively discussed elsewhere.

Sydney Glanville became obsessed with the Borley haunting, and he devoted much time and energy to his own investigation. As we have seen, he interviewed the Smiths and the Misses Bull. His son and daughter, Roger and Helen, became interested in the mystery, and Roger joined the teams of observers at the Rectory while Helen passed the lonely hours back home in Streatham experimenting with a planchette board (a thin wooden board on castors with a pencil fixed in a socket; the sitter touches the board with his fingers and allows it to run across a sheet of paper, thus producing automatic writing) in the hope of contacting the spirits who infested the Rectory.

Glanville was a strange mixture of the thorough and painstaking with the absurd and credulous. For example, he not only investigated the history of Borley and exploded the myth that there had a been a monastic foundation on or near the site of the Rectory; he also interviewed the Smiths (6 October 1937) and the Misses Bull (25 June 1938). But he was quite capable of taking the village gossip and malicious tales of the Misses Bull at face value, as the transcripts of the seances that were held at Borley make clear. The sitters, who usually included Glanville himself or his son Roger, and who used either a specially built seance table or a planchette, asked many leading questions that were inspired by the silly stories about the Bull family. The favourite themes were the alleged murder of a pregnant servant by the Rev. H.D.E. Bull and the alleged murder of the Rev. Harry Bull by his wife – the hated Ivy Bull, formerly Brackenbury:

Report of sitting held at B——— Rectory on 23 October 1937 just outside kitchen, starting at 9.55 p.m. ending 10.30 p.m. (A.J. Cuthbert, R.H. Glanville, M. Kerr-Pearse)

The sitting was begun at 9.55 p.m. and almost at once the table felt alive, and within two minutes was rocking backwards and forwards. During the sitting we all experienced an icy cold draught ... A.J. Cuthbert noticed an icy draught behind his ears ... Kerr-Pearse got the impression that there was a presence behind Cuthbert's right shoulder ... R.H. Glanville had the feeling that we were being watched ... the results obtained were as follows ...

Is someone there? Yes.
Who are you, will you spell your name? TFISME
Will you please repeat? TFISMONG
Are you a man or a woman? (uncertain)
Is your name Bull? No.
Is your name Foyster? No.
Have you lived here before? Yes
What is your age? 91
Have you a message for Marianne? No
Have you a message for anyone here? No.
Have you a message? Yes.
Will you please spell it? If chant mass light erel caedo.
Is it erel caedo? Yes.
Is erel an abbreviation? Yes.
Will you please continue? Blarnui.

Thus ended the first session. These seances were in the

tradition of the Foysters' eccentricities at Borley. When grown men hold solemn nocturnal conclave in a deserted house and wonder at icy draughts behind their ears, all is not well with them. Yet upon such cryptic replies as 'TFISMONG' is much of the Borley cult based; trained and serious investigators pored over these messages and claimed to make sense of them.

After this first session the experiment was repeated. Later that night the sitters began to recycle village gossip:

Then you are H.D.B.?* Yes
Did something unfortunate happen in the kitchen? Yes.
Did a servant girl die in your presence there? Yes.
Did she die a natural death? No.
Was she poisoned? (Hesitation)
Was she poisoned? No.
Was there a baby? Yes.

On 24 October, again in the hours of darkness, Harry Bull himself favoured the sitters with his presence:

Are you there? Yes.
Is that H.B.? Yes.
Have you a message for us? Yes.
Will you please spell it out? MIFOR
Do you mean misfortune? Yes.
Will you continue? AWIFE
Do you mean your wife? Yes.
Did you die in this house? Yes.
Did you die in the room we left? Yes.
Did you die naturally? No.
Were you poisoned? (Uncertain)
Were you poisoned? Yes.
Were you poisoned by your wife? Yes.

The interested reader may examine the full text of these exchanges in *The Locked Book of Borley Rectory*. The extracts I

* H.D.B. is Henry Dawson (Ellis) Bull.

have given should, however, be sufficient to illustrate how the powers of suggestion and the method of 'communication' – that is, the sitters put leading questions to the 'spirits' – tended to produce the results that the sitters desired. During other seances the shade of the Borley nun was contacted, and she identified herself as 'Mairie Lairre' from Le Havre. She was not English but French and had been brought to this country as the mistress of a member of the wealthy Waldegrave family who had once owned the manor of Borley. This new theory neatly solved the anachronisms of the original legend, and the problem presented by the absence of evidence for a monastic foundation at Borley was side-stepped.

The seance 'data', which was used by Harry Price when he wrote his Borley books, is rubbish. So are the theories about the nun. So too are all the 'communications' from members of the Bull family in which village gossip and the Misses Bull's slanders of their sister-in-law are rehearsed.

Price's tenancy ended on 19 May 1938. In November 1938 he made a BBC radio broadcast about the Borley 'mystery' and was contacted by the new owner, Captain Gregson, who reported his own spooky experiences. Gregson, the reader will remember, was the man who later burned down the Rectory for the fire-insurance money. This event was of no little interest to psychical researchers because an 'entity' had threatened to fire the house. That invaluable vade mecum of the spirit world, *The Locked Book of Borley*, contains the following:

> Does anyone want to speak to us? Yes.
>
> Who are you? Sunex Amures and one of the men mean to burn down the Rectory tonight at nine o'clock end of the haunting go to the Rectory and you will be able to see us enter into our own and under the ruins you will find bone of murdered wardens under the ruins means you to have proof of haunting of the Rectory at Borley the understanding of which game tells the story of the murder which happened there.
>
> In which room will the fire start? Over the hall. Yes yes you must go if you want proof.

VILLAGE FETE

Wednesday, June 21st

AT

BORLEY RECTORY

(By kind permission of Capt. W. H. Gregson).
(Sudbury or Long Melford Railway Stations).

MOST HAUNTED HOUSE
IN ENGLAND.

CONDUCTED TOURS OF HAUNTED ROOMS.

VISIT OF LONDON GHOST CLUB

President: Mr. HARRY PRICE.

Sideshows, Teas, etc.

OPENED BY

Mrs. R. A. BUTLER

at 3 p.m.   Grounds open 2.30 p.m.

Admission: Adults 6d., Parishioners 3d., Children 1d.

Printed by the " Suffolk & Essex Free Press," Sudbury.

Thus the stage was set for the advent of that fiery 'entity' Sunex Amures – and of the equally sulphurous fire-insurance investigators. Sadly the fire didn't happen on the night of the seance as Sunex Amures promised, but the next year on 27 February 1939 when Captain Gregson burned his own house down. Price and Gregson messed about in the charred remains as they tried to squeeze the last drops out of the story, and they even held a fête in the ruins on 21 June 1939. 'Conducted Tours of Haunted Rooms' were advertised in addition to sideshows and teas. Price and Gregson both made radio broadcasts about Borley, and Price installed 'observers' again. His first Borley book, *The Most Haunted House in England*, was published in 1940 and caused a sensation. Many educated men and women wrote to Price offering their contributions to the solution of the mystery, which was now held to depend on the history and identity of the dead nun.

The seances had provided Price with the hint (from the beyond) that the dead nun's bones were to be found in the cellars of the gutted building. These were found in 1943 during an excavation: Price had almost certainly put them there himself. His second Borley work, *The End of Borley Rectory*, appeared in 1945. Price died of a heart attack in 1948 and other wise men, trained and serious investigators, were left to carry the torch for the Most Haunted House in England.

But what of that strange couple, the Foysters? Where had they been while Mr Sydney H. Glanville and his friends sat rocking tables in the kitchen passage of the empty Rectory? The work of Price and the other investigators left the true mystery of Borley unsolved: the mystery of Lionel Algernon Foyster and his wife Marianne.

5

Hall of Fame

Through Price's books a veritable religious cult has grown up around Borley, a cult that is as strong today as it was fifty years ago when Price and the Rector of Borley-cum-Liston buried the bones of the murdered nun with full honours at Liston churchyard. Sadly, this Anglican rite does not appear to have quietened her tormented soul, as readers of a certain work on Borley will be aware. The nun still walks, more often in the churchyard now, but the Rev. Harry Bull, his father and the wronged domestics seem to have moved on to higher things. Clearly poor Harry's legal and probate problems have been sorted out on the 'other side', where he is now reunited with his charming sisters. Only the nun seems to be unhappy; she sends messages via mediums, pleading pathetically, 'Must I walk the earth forever?'

To which the only honest answer is, 'Yes, my dear, so long as there are psychical researchers left to write about you.' Perhaps the modern ghost hunters have added to her obvious distress. One writer has related how only a few years ago a man who had devoted much time to nocturnal vigils, in the best Borley tradition, was so shocked and surprised when at last the ghost of the nun appeared to him that instead of taking readings and measurements like a trained and serious investigator, or enquiring of her what steps might be taken to release her, he threw a brick at her. This seems churlish. To be murdered while incarnate is one thing; but to be obliged to perambulate in cold churchyards by night and have bricks thrown at one when discarnate is quite another. No wonder the poor nun complains of her fate.

In the early 1950s, the London Society for Psychical Research felt obliged to prosecute its own investigation of the alleged haunting of Borley Rectory. Three investigators were chosen to sift the evidence: Mrs K.M. Goldney, who had accompanied Price on his visit during the uproarious Foyster years, Dr Eric J. Dingwall, an academic in charge of the restricted collection (dirty books) at the British Library who rejoiced in the nickname 'Dirty Ding', and Trevor Hall. Their highly sceptical report, entitled *The Haunting of Borley Rectory*, was published in 1956.

Trevor Hall was the most determined and clear-minded of the three authors, and it fell to him to investigate the claims made by the Foysters. His first thought was to talk to them in person, but he soon found that this was impossible. No one knew what had become of them. From the surviving members of the Bull family – those sisters again – he found that Foyster had died in 1945 and that they had long ceased to have any dealings with his widow Marianne. Furthermore, Hall knew that Foyster had returned to England after twenty years in Canada to take up the Borley living, bringing Marianne with him – for all he knew Marianne might herself have been Canadian and have returned to her native country after her husband's death.

Hall's search for the elusive Marianne is as interesting as any fictional detective story, and was to end with the discovery not only of Marianne herself but also of fraud and deceit on an incredible scale, bigamy, adultery, blackmail and murder. Marianne Foyster was the true mystery of Borley. I have conducted my own research into Marianne's life (mainly in North America where she has lived since 1946), but must pay tribute to Hall; for without his early efforts, when the trail was still warm, Marianne would have vanished for ever into the wastes of North Dakota as she intended.

At the beginning of his search Hall had only two pieces of information about her. The first was from a Mrs Gay Taylor, who became interested in the Borley mystery (like many other people who had read Price's books) and who got in touch with Price himself. She said that during a telephone conversation

Price had told her, with some hilarity, that Marianne had become a GI bride. The implication of this was that Marianne had retured to North America, but to the United States, not Canada. The second was also from Mrs Gay Taylor. She claimed that a friend who had been at a Christmas house-party in Gloucestershire had met another guest who knew, or knew of, Marianne. When the Borley mystery was brought up in general conversation the woman said, with some emotion, that Marianne had enticed her weak-minded brother into a bigamous marriage while she had still been married to Foyster. This disastrous liaison had left her brother an emotional wreck. He had suffered a complete mental breakdown and now lived in seclusion in his devoted sister's care. She also expressed her conviction that Marianne had murdered Foyster.

Hall succeeded in tracing the marriage certificate of Marianne and the GI. Marianne's age at the time of the marriage was given as 32; but if she had been 32 in 1946, she would have been only 17 when Price met her at Borley, which was obviously impossible. There was an address on the certificate, and Hall took himself off to Ipswich to visit it.

Here another shock awaited him. The address was not only false, it was fictitious; 229 Ranelagh Road did not exist. Hall visited the registrar's office and pointed this out. Then he visited the addresses at which the Foysters had lived in the Thirties. These were known because Glanville (of *Locked Book* fame) and Harry Price had both corresponded with Foyster after his retirement, although neither had visited him.

Marianne's skeletons tumbled out of the closet with broad grins on their boney faces. At 102 Woodbridge Road East, where the Foysters had lived in the Thirties, no one was at home; but a helpful neighbour remembered them distinctly. There had been no Mr and Mrs Foyster, but a Mr and Mrs Fisher, who had sometimes taken out the wife's elderly father, an invalid named Mr Foyster, for rides in the car. The same tale was told by neighbours at Dairy Cottage, Rendlesham, north of the small Suffolk town of Woodbridge.

It became clear to Hall that the indoor diversions at Borley were not the least of the Foysters' escapades. He visited other addresses, including the one at Snape where the Foysters had lived between their days in Ipswich and Rendlesham. Here a terrible thing befell him. Whereas at Ipswich and Rendlesham the household had consisted of Mr and Mrs Fisher (Mrs Fisher was obviously Marianne; her neighbours remembered her well enough to give accurate descriptions of her appearance) and 'old Mr Foyster', who was a retired clergyman, at Snape there was just Mr and Mrs Foyster and their children!

Dark and terrible thoughts crowded in upon that trained and serious investigator as he grappled with the enigma of the Fishers, a conundrum as extraordinary as the identity and history of the Borley nun herself. How many Fishers were there? Did Marianne install lovers in her house with the agreement of old Mr Foyster, and require them, for reasons that remained dark to him, to call themselves Mr Fisher? Thus when there was a Mr Fisher in the house Marianne would become Mrs Fisher and the Rev. Foyster became her father. When she was between Fishers, she became Mrs Foyster again and the Rev. Foyster was restored as her husband.

But there was a catch. The name of the man on the wedding certificate wasn't Fisher but O'Neil (there was nothing on the certificate to identify this O'Neil as an American soldier); who was O'Neil? Was O'Neil a former Mr Fisher who after the Rev. Foyster's death had been allowed to revert to his true name and to become a husband in his own right? Had there been one Fisher all along? Or two Fishers? Or three, or even more?

Hall had not traced Marianne when the Borley report was published in 1956, but he had discovered how many Fishers there were. He had also discovered much about Marianne's life, not much of which was to her credit. Her eccentricity was matched by her husband's, whose accounts of the supernatural wonders they witnessed at Borley provided the foundation of the whole cult.

Trevor Hall has written his own account of his investigation which remains unpublished. He concentrates on his sagacity and his insight into the human personality and its twists and turns. I shall not tell any more of Hall's tale except when it impinges on the tale of Marianne and her husband. For the time has come to explain to the patient reader what was going on at Borley behind the smokescreen of ghosts and poltergeists.

6

Marianne's Early Life

Marianne was born on 26 January 1899 at 5, Guy Wood Cottages, Romiley, near Stockport in Cheshire. She was the second child of William Steele Shaw and Annie Elizabeth Shaw, née Woodyatt. Their elder child, a son named Geoffrey, had been born in 1897. Marianne's names on her birth certificate are given as Mary Anne Emily Rebecca; the more romantic 'Marianne' was a later invention.

Her father had had a chequered and unsuccessful career; he had been a schoolmaster at a small public school near Manchester, named Grafton House, but had left this job for reasons that remain unknown. He had tried to become a publican, at the Woodman Inn at Hyde, near Stockport, but was as unsuccessful at that as he had been as a schoolmaster. At the time of Marianne's birth he was eking out a precarious existence as a private tutor of shorthand and book-keeping, and his family lived in near poverty. No. 5, Guy Wood Cottages, which was then almost in the country, was in a terrace of very small houses with a single outside lavatory shared by the other families. William Shaw must have been a frustrated man, who had aspired to, but failed to achieve, better things. Perhaps his aspirations were transferred to his daughter, for in later life she was to regale various acquaintances with stories of the aristocratic splendour of her background, and of how she, Marianne, was a graduate of one of the Cambridge women's colleges – which she wasn't. The poor material circumstances of her childhood provided the catalyst for many later fantasies, including the wonderful tale that she was the daughter of the Countess von Kiergraff – late of Schleswig-Holstein – and the equally exotic Santiago Monk, an Englishman in the Chilean diplomatic service.

In Marianne's own words, 'Oh, I don't know, all my life I've been given to glamorising situations and propagandering; telling – as a child I used to make up stories that I was a princess, all kinds of silly things.' But her problem was not that she made up stories when she was a child, but that she went on doing it when she was an adult.

When she was two, her family moved to the other side of Manchester, to Lymm near Warrington; and it was here that the fateful meeting occurred between her and Lionel Algernon Foyster. What took William Shaw to Lymm is not known; but the family presumably continued to live in difficult material circumstances. In interviews Marianne has not provided much information about this period of her life, but has said that although her family was poor, she was not starved of love and affection by her parents.

It is hard to imagine a greater contrast of backgrounds than between Marianne's and Lionel Algernon's. He was born on 7 January 1878, in Hastings, into a comfortable family which had for many years provided the Church of England with clergymen. The Foysters, like the Bulls of Pentlow, were another Victorian ecclesiastical dynasty; because they were both rectors and patrons of the parishes they served, livings were passed from father to son.

Lionel Algernon's paternal grandfather was the Rev. Henry Samuel Foyster; according to the *Alumni Cantabrigienses*, Henry Samuel Foyster matriculated at Queen's College, Cambridge, at Michaelmas, 1811. In 1841 he was 'Lecturer at St Clement's and All Saints', Hastings'; in 1849 he became Rector of All Saints', presumably at the instance of his brother John, over ten years his senior, who was patron of that living. Henry Samuel was Rector of All Saints' until his death on 6 July 1862; his brother John was Rector of St Clement's until 1855, when he 'disappears from the *Clergy List*'.

The younger brother, Henry Samuel, had two sons who became clergymen and who in their turn held the livings of St

Clement's and All Saints'. The elder of these was the Rev. Henry Brereton Foyster, who was born in 1834, went to Trinity College, Cambridge and was Rector and patron of St Clement's from 1801 to 1906, when he handed over to *his* son, the Rev. Henry Charles Brereton Foyster; and the younger son was Lionel Algernon's father, George Alfred, who also went to Trinity and became Rector and patron of All Saints' from 1862 to 1904. He died almost exactly a year after his elder brother, in 1911.

This genealogy is not just of general interest; later in this book the question of whether Lionel Algernon Foyster was, in effect, held captive by Marianne for almost a decade, including a period of over two years when he was supposed to be locked up in the roof of a small bungalow in Ipswich (the house that was visited in Woodbridge Road East by Hall), must be considered. Whether Foyster was under duress is of vital importance in piecing together the relationship between him and Marianne. Here we simply note that his father and uncle, the two Hastings rectors, both had large families, and that Foyster had many comparatively wealthy and influential relatives to whom he could have appealed had he been in trouble. In the 1911 edition of *Crockford's Clerical Directory*, five Foysters, including Lionel Algernon himself, are listed; they are all related! Apart from Lionel Algernon, they are his father and three cousins, who were rectors in Norfolk, Sussex and Hastings. There are four Foysters in the 1933 edition – again, all are related.

His father, George Alfred Foyster, married Adelaide Julia Tillard, the third daughter of Philip Tillard, JP, of Stukely Hall in Huntingdon. Thus through his mother's family Lionel Algernon had another set of relations of considerable social standing and influence, at least some of whom would have helped him had he so requested during the period of his supposed imprisonment by his wife.

Lionel Algernon was the fourth son of the Rev. George Alfred Foyster and the only one to follow the family's clerical tradition (there were also two sisters, Hilda and Adelaide). He was educated at Bilton Grange and Haileybury, and entered Pembroke College, Cambridge, in 1897. Pembroke were unable to inform me what he read, but confirmed that he was granted a degree by 'special examination' at Easter, 1900. From Cambridge he went to Wells Theological College, and then to his first curacy at Heptonstall in Yorkshire. He was ordained deacon at Wakefield Cathedral in 1903 and priest in 1904.

When his uncle retired from St Clement's in 1906, the living passed to his eldest son. His father, the Rector of the other family living, All Saints', resigned in 1904; he was also patron, and if he had wanted to, and if Lionel Algernon had wanted to accept, he could surely have passed his living on to *his* son; and yet Lionel Algernon stayed in Yorkshire, as curate of Heptonstall from 1903 to 1905. His father retired to Guise House, at Aspley Guise in Bedfordshire, where he died on 11 December 1911.

Why didn't Lionel Algernon take the family living? Why did he remain in Yorkshire and then move to Oughtrington in Cheshire in 1905, to another curacy? For not only did he remain a curate, his superior was his brother-in-law, the Rev. Edmund Peel Wethered, who had married his sister Adelaide. The living of All Saints' would surely have been highly desirable, and it was within his family's gift. It is not unreasonable to conclude that there was some scandal or family difficulty involving Lionel Algernon, which not only persuaded his father that he could not be allowed to take over All Saints', but also led to his serving his second curacy under the watchful eye of his brother-in-law at Oughtrington.

That this was the case is further indicated by Lionel Algernon's next move: to New Brunswick in 1910, as Rector of Hardwicke with Bay du Vin. Today 85 per cent of New Brunswick is still forested; many parts of the province remain backward and remote. Furthermore, Bay du Vin lies on the coast that faces the Gulf of St Lawrence, and in 1910 it must have been inhospitable and backward, with a hinterland of forest, lumber camps and primitive settlements. Foyster was in effect engaged in missionary work; the people of New Brunswick were predominantly rural, and composed of various ethnic groups, the Anglo-Saxon Loyalists, the Francophone Acadians, and later Scandinavian and Central European settlers. A greater contrast with the life that he might reasonably have expected in the family living at genteel Hastings can hardly be imagined.

I have been unable to find out why Foyster took himself off to the Canadian backwoods. There is, of course, the perfectly reasonable explanation that he simply wanted to work abroad. One of his brothers had taken himself off to India, in the Indian Civil Service, and died of typhoid at Moultan in the Punjab in 1897. On the other hand Foyster's later conduct, when he was back in England and married to Marianne, indicates that he was a sexual pervert. The evidence for this will be presented later. It seems likely that he had got himself into trouble with his father early in his career through some sexual misdemeanor. Exactly what he did must remain a mystery, though the fact that he remained unmarried until he was forty-two, his strange choice of wife (Marianne), and his incredible domestic arrangements after his marriage suggest a tendency towards voyeurism and paedophilia.

When the Rev. Lionel Algernon Foyster befriended, or was befriended by, Marianne's family, he was the curate of Oughtrington, which is only about a mile away from Lymm where they were living. He actually baptised his future wife on 19 June 1906, when she was seven years old. He seems to have become fascinated by the pretty little girl with raven-black hair and startlingly pale skin who liked to make up silly stories about being a princess. Marianne has never volunteered what she made of him at this stage of their relationship.

Foyster's baptism of Marianne was to have consequences much later, when – according to Marianne – he is alleged to have concluded that their later marriage was invalid because his sacramental role at her baptism made him her 'Spiritual Father', a relationship that precluded Holy Matrimony; this, according to Marianne, was her husband's – or 'Spiritual Father's' theological justification for his wife's – or 'Spiritual Daughter's' – having sexual relationships with other men after they were married.

Foyster once said of himself that if he had not become a cleric, he would have become an actor; he is said to have loved plays and play-acting (a predeliction that would have equipped him quite wonderfully to sit on the selection committees of the modern Church of England, at which aspiring clergymen are sat down in front of, say, a country vicar and the manager of a biscuit factory, who pretend to be bereaved or terminally ill, while the postulant exhibits his prowess by consoling them. This is called 'role-playing').

Unfortunately there were no such outlets for creative energy in Foyster's day. Perhaps Foyster and Marianne, the lonely curate and the pretty little girl, were able to enter into each other's brightly coloured fantasy worlds: worlds that would eventually engulf not only their creators, but also many other unfortunates with whom they were associated. That Foyster became fascinated by Marianne to the extent of being obsessed with her is undeniable. People who knew them much later, as a married couple, reported that he adored and doted upon his young wife, that he was jealous of her affection and company, and that he became restless and unhappy if she was away from the house for more than a few hours. Marianne said that her husband 'wanted her around him like a doll if nothing else'. This period of Foyster the curate playing Charles Dodgson to Marianne's Alice Liddell ended when he went to the Canadian backwoods in 1910, though the Shaw family and the former curate kept in touch.

The Shaw family too moved west in 1907, to Northern Ireland, where William Shaw obtained a post as time-keeper for the British Portland Cement Company. Nothing more is known of Marianne's early life until 1914, when she went on holiday in Scotland and stayed with the family of a clerk, Harold Giffard Greenwood, who worked for the same company as her father. Greenwood, who was aged twenty-one, accompanied her; and when she returned, she announced to her parents that not only was she married (the civil ceremony was registered at Stranraer), but also that she was pregnant, or likely to be so. On 12 November 1914, Greenwood and Marianne were married again in St Anne's Cathedral, Belfast. On the marriage certificate her age is stated as seventeen when she was in fact fifteen. Marianne later gave false information on many official forms, for example, by reducing her age by a good fourteen years on the certificate of her marriage to the GI in 1945; the certificate of her marriage to Greenwood is the only instance of her *increasing* her age. Her father's occupation is stated as 'schoolmaster', which, though he once had been, he was no longer. This suggests that Marianne's tendency to fantasise and lie was reinforced by the pathetic dishonesty of her parents as they tried to cling to the outward appearances of gentility.

With financial help from Greenwood's parents – his father was a clergyman – the young couple set up home not far from where the Shaws were living, near Larne. The child was born on 19 April 1915 and was named Ian Geoffrey William. Only six weeks after the birth Greenwood ran off, never to be seen again; various stories are told of his subsequent career, none of which have been verified. He is said to have gone to England, or to Australia; he is said to have died in England; he is said to have died in Australia; he is said to have married again ... and so on.

There never appears to have been a divorce, though her father had a solicitor draw up a document of legal separation. If there was no divorce, Marianne's later marriage to Foyster was of course bigamous. The important question of how much Foyster knew or guessed about his dream-child's past when he proposed to her himself in 1922, will be discussed shortly.

Marianne's son was brought up by his grandparents. Marianne later claimed, during an interview in America in 1958, that she was distressed by this because her mother took over the baby and wouldn't let her care for him. The son used his mother's maiden name throughout his life, calling himself Ian Geoffrey William Shaw, and was later a source of much information about his mother's life, having no scruples about exposing her wilder and more eccentric activities which, but for him, would have been known only to her and to the shattered victims of her cruel impostures and deceptions. According to the son's account, Marianne worked in munitions factories in England during the First World War while he remained in his grandparents' care. She embarked upon a long series of affairs with a wide variety of men. When she returned to Larne she continued to behave in the same way, becoming, in his own words, 'the talk of the town'. She also reverted to her maiden name and once again became Marianne Shaw.

Meanwhile, out in Canada, Lionel Algernon had moved from

Hardwicke in 1918 to become Missionary-in-charge of Gordon with Lorne – in another remote location – and from there to Salmonhurst in 1921, as Missioner of Drummond. Salmonhurst and Drummond are in the wild country near the border between New Brunswick and Maine. Examination of a map of Canada's Atlantic Provinces will show just how remote and isolated they are; the lifeline to civilisation was the railway that passed through nearby New Denmark and which went on to Fredericton, one of the few substantial towns in New Brunswick.

It was from Salmonhurst that Foyster wrote to Marianne in 1922, proposing marriage. Marianne accepted, and on 22 August 1922 Lionel Algernon Foyster, aged forty-four, married Marianne Emily Rebecca Shaw, aged twenty-three, at Salmonhurst. Although Marianne gave her correct age on the marriage certificate, her state was described as 'a spinster of no occupation'. There was no mention of her being a divorcee. Why did Foyster propose marriage to this extraordinary woman, and how much did he know about her life in Ireland?

Mrs Lionel Algernon Foyster

All the accounts of Marianne's life that have so far appeared have been by committed psychical researchers. They are therefore suspect. These authors' interest in Marianne is secondary to their interest in establishing her as a reliable witness of the Borley wonders, or otherwise. This means that they are either too vicious in their assessment of her, since they wish to debunk Borley by rubbishing her character (which is not difficult), or they wish to rehabilitate Borley by rehabilitating her (which is difficult). The late Trevor Hall is the principal example of the first kind, while Iris Owen and Pauline Mitchell are spectacular examples of the second. Both tend to lose sight of the world outside the hot-house of psychical research; when they are not discussing poltergeists they seem quite lost, and appear to lack any insight into the characters of their witnesses.

Hall, who devoted much of his time and energy to a search for the elusive Marianne after she had fled England for the United States, would countenance no good of her; she was, in his words, a nymphomaniac and a pathological liar, and her husband was a credulous old fool and a helpless victim in her hands. Owen and Mitchell, on the other hand, in their article published in the *Journal of the Society for Psychical Research*, try to present an absurdly charitable picture of Marianne, based on an interview with the lady herself in 1979. This time the story is that the Foysters were a devoted couple, that Foyster knew all about her past before she married him, and that her past was not as bad as her son made out. Owen and Mitchell simply ignore the evidence to the contrary, and happily rehabilitate Marianne, not for her own sake, be it noted, but for the sake of the poltergeists she is alleged to have witnessed at Borley.

None of this will do. It is another example of psychical researchers, who are forever crying out for open-mindedness, doctoring the facts to suit their theories – or rather their prejudices, for they rarely, if ever, have theories worthy of the name.

*

Foyster returned to the United Kingdom on leave on several occasions during his Canadian service, and he visited the Shaws in Northern Ireland. According to Marianne's son Ian, her parents were careful to accommodate him well outside Larne so that none of the gossip and scandal reached his ears. Ian Shaw claimed that he was always passed off as his mother's younger brother, and that Foyster knew nothing about her marriage to Greenwood and subsequent career. If this be true, these pretences were obviously maintained in the correspondence between the Shaws and Foyster when he was in Canada. In any case, Foyster couldn't have visited the Shaws very often between 1915 and 1918 because of the restrictions imposed on civilian passenger shipping by the German U-boat campaign.

In interviews in 1958 with an American private investigator named A. Robert Swanson Marianne confirmed at least part of this story.

> *Swanson*: Why did you introduce Ian as your younger brother to Lionel?
>
> *Marianne*: He was always known as that. My parents kept him from the time of his birth and he didn't live with me until he came out to Canada for a visit. My older brother Geoffrey had been out there to visit and then Ian came because he suffered from asthma and it was thought that the air out there would be good for him.
>
> *Swanson*: Did Lionel ever know that he was your son?
>
> *Marianne*: No, he never did.

These transcripts were available to Owen and Mitchell when they wrote their article. But their version of events reads as follows: 'Lionel Foyster was, of course, completely aware of her marital status, or otherwise, when he suggested she joined him in Canada and become his wife. They had corresponded frequently for some time, and she had told him about her marriage, the baby, and the subsequent events.'

This is in itself a very odd statement; what do the authors mean by 'her marital status, or otherwise'? Are they implying that if Marianne had not in fact been legally divorced from Greenwood, Foyster would have been prepared to marry her none the less?

Yet only a few paragraphs later, the same authors make an incredible statement about Foyster's deeply religious views of matrimony:

> Marianne tells us that at their wedding reception, Lionel boasted to Dr Smithers, who performed the marriage ceremony, that he, Lionel, had baptized Marianne when she was a baby.* He was disturbed by Smithers's response to that information. According to Marianne, Dr Smithers said that marriage, although valid in the eyes of the law, would not be regarded as valid in the eyes of the church, as Lionel stood in the relationship of a spiritual father to Marianne. Marianne says that this shocked Lionel very much. Dr Smithers's comment seems very strange to us, but Marianne assured us that is it true. What is important of course is, that if Lionel Foyster believed that as far as the church was concerned his marriage was not valid, this might explain his subsequent acceptance both of Marianne's 'flings' as she described them, and of her interim 'marriage' to Fisher.†

This is nonsense. The authors deliberately use anodyne forms of words. The later marriage to Fisher was not in any sense

---

* She was not a baby when Foyster baptised her; she was 7 years old.
† This will be discussed in detail later.

'interim'; it was solemnised in a Roman Catholic church, and Marianne perjured herself not only in the eyes of the law, but also, from the point of view of a committed Catholic, in the eyes of God.

Furthermore, Foyster has been described by people who knew him both socially and in his professional capacity as a deeply religious, almost saintly, man. He was also, it is worth noting, of the Anglican Catholic persuasion. If he had truly held to the principles that might be expected of a deeply religious Anglo-Catholic cleric, it would surely have troubled his conscience to marry a divorcee. According to this account, it troubled him not at all, but he was greatly disturbed by the silly idea (which has no basis in doctrine or practice) that because he had married the woman whom he had once baptized, their marriage was somehow invalid. To suggest that Foyster believed that this also justified his wife's extra-marital affairs is stretching credulity to the utmost. Finally, Foyster's domestic arrangements after the couple had returned to England, when he not only tolerated but actively assisted with the installation of his wife's lovers in his own home while he pretended to be her elderly father, suggest that his view of sexual morality was rather unusual, especially for a saintly and deeply religious clergyman. Owen and Mitchell's article is a beautiful example of the distortions peddled by psychical researchers in defence of their vested interests.

Why would a forty-four-year-old clergyman, who had buried himself for twelve years in the Canadian backwoods, suddenly propose marriage to a woman he either hardly knew or who, he realised, was deeply disturbed and a somewhat unconventional candidate for a missionary's wife? Even psychical researchers couldn't suppose that after careful consideration of her attributes and career, Foyster concluded that Marianne was ideally suited to be his helpmate in his work of spreading the word to remote lumber camps in New Brunswick. And why did Marianne, who had already made something of a mess of things through her unrestrained quest for sexual gratification, accept?

It is said of the Rev. Foyster that he was so deeply religious that he believed in the propriety of sexual intercourse, even between husband and wife, only when they both consciously desired to conceive a child, the Catholic practice of what is known as Matrimonial Chastity. If this was indeed the case, one can only say that Lionel and Marianne each were remarkably unfortunate in their choice of spouse.

If Marianne had really become 'the talk of the town' in Larne, both she and her parents must have experienced considerable social difficulties; and Marianne must have caused her parents a great deal of inconvenience and anguish. In these circumstances, even Foyster's somewhat eccentric proposal, which offered Marianne the opportunity of a respectable marriage, and a new life in a distant country where she could leave her unsavoury past behind, would have seemed like the answer to a desperate prayer. Marianne may have come under pressure from her family to accept. If so, and if Foyster didn't know what kind of woman his dream-child had become, Marianne's parents were being somewhat unfair to him; it was less than charitable for Marianne to marry him without giving the poor man some idea of what he was in for. It is significant that Marianne practised exactly this kind of deception upon other men with whom she later become involved: that is, she married them after adopting a false character, and in the case of the mentally unstable commercial traveller Fisher, whom she bigamously married in Ipswich in 1935 and of whom much more will be told later, after adopting a false identity. If Marianne's parents not only colluded with her in deceiving Foyster but actively encouraged her, it is not unreasonable to conclude that they had encouraged her to deceive in other situations. Such a family background, combined with Marianne's own tendency to fantasy and her fertile imagination, produced a pathological liar who was, later in life, unable to tell the unadorned truth even when it was clearly in her own interest to do so.

This situation and the marriage are not incompatible with Lionel's knowing a certain amount about her chequered past prior to his proposal. If Foyster was in regular touch with the Shaws, they probably confided at least some of their family problems to their clergyman friend. Foyster may have been motivated in part by charity, and may have offered to marry her because he too realised that this gave his idol a chance to begin again in a new country. That he was infatuated with her is consistent with this, because not even a saintly man would make such an offer to a woman such as Marianne if he were not deeply emotionally involved with her.

Only Marianne knows the answer to this riddle; and Marianne tells a different version every time she is interviewed. The correspondence between her and her future husband, if it still exists, would provide the answer, but this has not been available. The only clues are offered by curious features of the relationship between Marianne and Lionel as man and wife, and by their unconventional domestic arrangements after they had returned to England.

*

The known facts about the Foysters' residence in Canada are as follows. They lived at Salmonhurst Rectory until 1927, when Foyster became Rector of Sackville. The registers of the Bishop of Fredericton (Bishop Richardson) contain the following entry:

> Jan 15th 1927. The Rev. L.A. Foyster (Resignation). The Bishop accepted the resignation of the Rev. L.A. Foyster from the parish (mission) of Drummond to take effect from Feby 7th. 1927.

Sackville was a far more civilised place than Salmonhurst, for it was a substantial town and the site of the famous Mt Allison University. According to Bishop Richardson's register:

> Feby 26th 1927. Rev. Lionel Algernon Foyster (Institution). The Bishop on February 13th. instituted the Rev. Lionel Algernon Foyster into the Rectory of St Paul's church in the county of Westmorland.

This was to be Foyster's last appointment in Canada, and in 1929 he and Marianne left Sackville and for a short time lived in St John. Foyster returned to England in order to find a living (he was now unemployed) and was offered Borley by his cousins, the Bulls, who were the patrons. The Foysters moved back to England in 1930, and after a short time living with or near the Bulls in Great Cornard, they moved into Borley Rectory on 16 October. Bishop Richardson's registers supply only the following information:

> July 22nd 1929. Rev. L.A. Foyster (Resignation). The Bishop accepted the resignation of the Rev. L.A. Foyster (to take effect Sept 15th next) from Parish of Sackville.

> Sept 9th 1929. Rev. L.A. Foyster (Leave of absence). The Bishop, Sept 7th 1929, granted leave of absence from his duties in the space of twelve months to Rev. Lionel Algernon Foyster.

The only information about the Foysters' life in Canada, apart from the above sources and the contradictory statements made by Marianne herself, has come from her son, Ian, who joined them at Salmonhurst in 1925. According to him if Marianne's intention had been to give up her old ways and to start over again she was spectacularly unsuccessful. Ian Shaw's statements must be treated cautiously, because he hated his mother and didn't hesitate to reveal the most damaging facts about her. His statements are uncorroborated. I have not found any hint of the scandals he reported in either the diocesan records of Fredericton or in contemporary newspapers. On the other hand, what Ian said about his mother is plausible when her activities in England, for which documentary evidence exists, are considered.

According to Ian Greenwood Shaw, Marianne soon became involved with other men in Canada. At Salmonhurst her list of conquests is alleged to include a young Anglican clergyman named Hall and a Roman Catholic priest, Father du Parc. She also began to flirt – and that is a most appropriate word to use – with the Roman Catholic Faith. This was perhaps stimulated by her environment in which 85 per cent of the population were French-Canadian Catholics. Later she would weave Roman

1. Borley Rectory

2. Borley Rectory after the fire

3. Marianne Foyster, circa 1922

4. Harry Price *(left)* at Borley with Marianne and Lionel Foyster *(centre)*

5. Marianne with bottle

6. Marianne with Mrs Fenton of Wimbledon

7. Marianne in front of Borley with baby
John Fisher

8. Henry Francis Fisher

9. Marianne *(2nd from right)* in frontier costume at a party in Jamestown

Catholicism into her fantastic stories about her background and antecedents. She even contracted one of her bigamous marriages in a Roman Catholic church.

The scandals caused by Marianne's behaviour are alleged to have greatly displeased the Bishop of Fredericton (this comes from Ian Shaw and the reader should note that no records about this survive in the diocese of Fredericton), to whose notice they came; her son alleges that she attempted suicide by swallowing lysol after one disastrous liaison. Foyster's health was also in decline. The rheumatoid arthritis that was later to cripple him appeared while he was at Salmonhurst, and according to Marianne he suffered a heart attack while swimming. Ian said that Foyster moved from Salmonhurst to Sackville because of the scandals and difficulties caused by his wife's behaviour, but he is just as likely to have moved from a rural to an urban parish because of his deteriorating health.

At Sackville Marianne soon got herself into trouble again. Eventually the Bishop of Fredericton could stand no more, and he asked Foyster to leave the diocese. Foyster then moved to St John and in due course obtained the living of Borley. According to Ian Shaw, the following incident occurred while he and his mother were living alone in St John (Foyster was in England); it is worth repeating because it nicely illustrates Marianne's peculiar character.

Marianne was involved in a minor collision with a car driven by a Major Forbes-Mitchell of the Government Survey Office. Ian was with his mother and witnessed not only the crash but its aftermath. Marianne introduced herself to the Major as Mrs von Kiergraff, a name that crops up several times in the history of her impostures. Because Foyster was away, Marianne was able to improve upon her first meeting with Major Forbes-Mitchell, visiting his house and receiving expensive presents from him. It all came to an end when, while inspecting the Major's gun collection, Ian smeared gun-oil on his jacket. The Major gallantly insisted on having it cleaned; unfortunately he found a letter in one of the pockets with Ian's name and address on it. He became suspicious and later asked Ian what school he attended. The Major phoned the school, established who Ian and his mother really were, and complained to the police. The acquaintance between Marianne and Major Forbes-Mitchell ended unpleasantly, with the return of the presents and a certain amount of scandal.

Another of Ian's stories – which cannot, unfortunately, be corroborated – is that his mother claimed to have witnessed poltergeist activity, not only at Salmonhurst Rectory, but at the Rectory in Sackville. This appears to be a foretaste of the wild days at Borley, where household objects flew through the air, or vanished only to appear somewhere else, and where she claimed to have been hurled from her bed by 'unseen forces'.

It is perhaps no coincidence that her first flirtation with poltergeists should have been in Canada; for Amherst, in Nova Scotia, was the site of perhaps one of the most famous hauntings of all time, in which a young woman named Esther Cox claimed to have heard mysterious voices (as Marianne did at Borley), to have witnessed the movement of household objects and furniture without visible cause (Marianne claimed to see such things at Borley), and to have seen apparitions invisible to everyone else (Marianne made exactly the same claims at Borley!).

The Amherst Mystery, as it is often called, was as celebrated in its day as Borley was to become over half a century later. A man named Walter Hubble wrote a book about it, just as Harry Price was later to write about Borley. It was a bestseller. Sackville, which is not far from the border with Nova Scotia, is also not far from Amherst. The Foysters would have heard tell of the great Amherst mystery. Furthermore, when writing his own account of the haunting of Borley (*Fifteen Months in a Haunted House*), Foyster named one of his characters 'Teed'; Esther Cox's brother-in-law, in whose house she lived and witnessed the haunting, was named Teed.

I believe the Foysters left Canada in 1930 for three reasons. Foyster had lost much of his private fortune in the Wall Street Crash of 1929, his health was worsening, and the Bishop of Fredericton had finally lost patience with Marianne. Foyster's decline was not only physical but mental. According to Marianne he was 'always off his rocker'. More charitably she explained, 'I don't mean that he was a lunatic. He was suffering from a form of heart trouble that deprives the brain of – well, whatever it is that causes it. He was very, very forgetful all his life, but more so towards the later years of his life. He would place things down and wouldn't be able to find them, then when he found them again he'd say that "The Things" had carried it around.'

'The Things' was Foyster's pet-name for the poltergeists. Marianne's statement not only explains why the Foysters' rectories in Canada were also infested with 'poltergeists', but disposes of many of the wonders recorded by Foyster in his *Summary of Experiences*. Many of the events which caused him such consternation can be explained simply by his failing memory; the reader will recall that Foyster was dumbfounded by the miraculous appearance of a lavender bag on a mantelpiece which then mysteriously moved to his pocket, and the sudden and wholly inexplicable appearance of a pot of fresh tea in the Rectory dining room.

Assuming that Ian's account of his mother's escapades in Canada is true – and they are certainly in character – the problem immediately arises of determining what, if anything, her husband made of it all. He would hear nothing against his adored wife, not even from his spiritual superior, the Bishop of Fredericton. He is said to have attributed the scandalous stories to malicious gossips and mean-minded people who were jealous of Marianne's charm and good looks and who deliberately misrepresented her kindness and friendliness to lonely men. This suggests that Foyster was either incredibly blind and stupid, or that he so adored his wife, and was so infatuated with her, that he would risk everything rather than be parted from her.

I shall return to this question in a later chapter, after more of the Foysters' story has been told, and give what I believe to be the most plausible explanation of his behaviour including not only his public defence of his wife and his apparent toleration of her affairs with other men, but also his proposal of marriage.

When the Foysters returned to England in 1930, they left Ian behind to finish his education; he did not return until 1933, when he joined the bizarre household that had grown up at

Borley. With them they brought a little girl named Adelaide, whom they had adopted in Canada after her mother had died in childbirth and her father had been killed in a farm accident. Foyster had baptized her himself at Sackville. One can't help wondering whether he would have proposed marriage to her as well, if he had lived longer. Adelaide had a terrible life with the Foysters, and played an important (though innocent) role in the development of the haunting of Borley Rectory.

8

Fifteen Months in a Haunted House

With their arrival at Borley in October 1930 the Foysters step out of the shadows and become substantial figures (Plate 4). Marianne was a handsome, dark-haired woman of medium height. Foyster was tall, thin and slightly stooped. Foyster was already suffering from chronic arthritis, but Marianne, in contrast, was young, healthy and active. The only complaint from which she is known to have suffered was gynaecological, and (according to Marianne) she had had surgical treatment for it in Canada – probably at Amherst. She suffered from heavy menstrual flows, and the treatment was apparently connected with this condition.

The reader of the popular works on Borley will learn that by 1931 the household included the mysterious M. François d'Arles, the F. de Arles of Foyster's *Summary of Experiences* behind whose bedroom door a paint-pot that defied all rational explanation appeared. François d'Arles rented the Rectory cottage, and his son, also named François, provided some companionship for Adelaide. What the reader of the popular works will *not* learn is that his father was also providing some companionship of a less innocent kind for Marianne.

Briefly, it appears that François d'Arles, who was not a Frenchman but an Englishman and a former London street vendor who sold flowers outside Stoke Newington cemetery, and whose real name was Frank Pearless, was a lover whom Marianne had succeeded in installing at the Rectory. Although d'Arles lived in the Rectory cottage, which was close by, he spent much time with the Foysters, taking meals with them and often sleeping in the Rectory itself.

D'Arles's true role at Borley is ignored in the bulk of the literature, and in *all* the popular works on the subject. The motives of these authors in suppressing the matter are hard to understand; perhaps they feel that it would detract in some way from the credibility of those persons who claimed to have witnessed poltergeist effects. If so, their integrity and impartiality is at once suspect. Furthermore, even the few investigators who have recognised d'Arles's role present a most implausible explanation of Foyster's attitude to his domestic situation; they present Foyster as a credulous and eccentric man who blindly trusted his wife, whom he adored and of whom he would hear no wrong, and who was led a long way up the garden path. This simply will not do; it just doesn't make sense.

*

The established facts about the Foysters' life at Borley are as follows. They moved into the Rectory, with little Adelaide, on 16 October 1930. According to Foyster's written accounts of what happened, Marianne soon began to hear strange noises including mysterious voices, and saw apparitions of the late Harry Bull – not the nun. Soon household objects were being hurled about, Marianne was being thrown out of bed by unseen forces – whatever an unseen force is – and a ghost was writing messages on the walls of an upstairs passage. In March 1931 Frank Pearless, aka François d'Arles, came into residence at the Rectory cottage, bringing with him his son, François junior, who was about the same age as Adelaide.

The respectable explanation of this arrangement was that the Foysters had placed an advertisement in a newspaper – given variously as *The Times* or *Church Times* – for a companion for Adelaide, and d'Arles had replied. Another version has d'Arles himself placing the advert. At Borley, Pearless-d'Arles was Marianne's lover – or sexual partner. There was no love affair, for Marianne and d'Arles seem to have hated and distrusted each other. Although the new phase of the haunting was well under way before d'Arles appeared at Borley, it continued with increasing violence afterwards. There were many witnesses to the 'phenomena', including the Foysters' neighbours, Sir George and Lady Whitehouse of Arthur Hall and their nephew Edwin, who came to stay with them in June 1931. In October Harry Price visited Borley and accused Marianne of faking the effects. In January 1932 the Marks Tey Spiritualist group visited Borley, and the 'phenomena' ceased abruptly. In January next year Marianne's son, Ian, arrived from Canada and became friendly with d'Arles during his brief residence at the Rectory; according to Ian, d'Arles told him that Marianne was a 'sexual maniac', that the poltergeist effects had been faked by Marianne and himself, and that he, d'Arles, had advised Marianne that things were getting out of hand, which was why they took the opportunity presented by the Spiritualist group's visit to 'exorcise' the ghosts.

In February 1933 Marianne opened a florist's shop in Wimbledon, Jonquille et Cie, at 20a, Worple Road. This is now the site of a Sainsbury's supermarket. Marianne came to Borley only at weekends during this period, and she and d'Arles lived as man and wife in Wimbledon, in the flat above the shop. The business failed in late 1934, and Marianne broke with d'Arles. She then began to spend as much time in Ipswich as she had in Wimbledon and found a replacement for d'Arles, a mentally unstable commercial traveller named Henry Francis Fisher, with whom she contracted a bigamous marriage in St Pancras Roman Catholic Church, Ipswich, on 23 February 1935. During this entire period Foyster was in mental and physical decline, and after collapsing in the pulpit at Borley he retired because of his ill health. The Foysters left Borley in October 1935; they lived in Ipswich with Fisher, who believed that Foyster was Marianne's elderly, invalid father.

*

What sense can be made of this incredible story? The simplest explanation is that Foyster, because of his poor health, was no longer able – if indeed he had ever been able – to satisfy his wife's vast sexual appetite, and that it was found necessary to call in a substitute, a surrogate husband, in the form of d'Arles. Trevor Hall further explained this as follows. Foyster adored his wife. He had already refused to hear any wrong of her in Canada, and continued to do so when Harry Price accused her of fraud. Marianne's own statements, however, must be taken into account. During the interview with Swanson, the American private detective, she was questioned about this:

> *Swanson*: But you told me a few moments ago that Lionel suspected, or that you had told Lionel, that you had relations with d'Arles?
> *Marianne*: Yes, I did.
> *Swanson*: And what did he say when you told him that?
> *Marianne*: He said that I was a naughty girl.
> *Swanson*: But you continued having relations with him, with d'Arles?
> *Marianne*: Yes.

Clearly if Foyster had shut his mind to his wife's involvement with other men and refused to accept the evidence, including the displeasure of his Bishop, he was no longer able to do so at Borley. If at some stage Marianne's conduct was so extreme that Foyster was no longer able to ignore her infidelities, this implies that there was not only a discontinuity in their relationship and a domestic crisis, but a severe emotional upheaval for Foyster himself. We must not forget that everyone who knew them as a couple has emphasised his devotion to her and his jealousy of her time and attention.

Yet no evidence of a sudden domestic crisis exists. Nor does Foyster's behaviour indicate any sudden crisis; his oddities can be accounted for by his declining mental health and his eccentricity, of which there is ample evidence, including the testimony of Marianne herself. Again, the story that Foyster was a credulous dupe, who vividly illustrated the truth of the old saying 'There's no fool like an old fool' simply does not account for the facts. There can be no doubt that Foyster was a willing and active accomplice in his wife's infidelities.

François d'Arles (or Frank Pearless) is hardly the kind of man who would regularly read the personal columns of *The Times*, still less the *Church Times*. The story of his having replied to an advert in one of those papers is absurd. It is not unreasonable to conclude that Marianne had met him somewhere, probably in London, and identified him as a suitable sexual partner. Foyster consented to his installation at Borley, and the story of the newspaper advert – there might have been an advert placed in a paper for cosmetic reasons – was to camouflage what was really happening from friends and relations.

That this is what happened is supported by the fact that Foyster later lived in the same house as a man whom his wife had bigamously married, and pretended to be his wife's elderly father. This calls the nature of Foyster's religious beliefs and his sexuality into question. Whether or not he was a saintly man in the discharge of his parochial duties, whether or not he made conventional public pronouncements about the Christian faith, his view of sexual morality was clearly unusual, and so was his own sexuality.

*

We are now in a position to understand the origin and development of the relationship between Foyster and Marianne. I believe that in a sense Foyster was deeply religious. Marianne made a revealing statement in a letter to her son Ian:

> At last he got very old and could not see anything without it being a sin. He was hollering about sin over and over when he collapsed.

The event she was referring to was Lionel's final collapse in the pulpit at Borley. The evidence has already been presented for supposing that Foyster had committed some early indiscretion as a result of which he was denied the family living in Hastings and finally went into a kind of exile in the Canadian forests. He probably had an abnormal sex urge towards children. This would explain the intense relationship that grew up between him and the little Marianne whom he baptized and his later fixation on her. Marianne evidently came to sexual maturity early and had a substantial sex drive. If they corresponded, as they are supposed to have done, and shared the play-acting and fantasy worlds that both enjoyed, an explicitly sexual element may well have crept into their confidences during her late adolescence and early womanhood; she did, after all, show an obsessive sexual interest in men that appears to have precluded almost any form of relationship other than that of deceiver and deceived.

People who knew the Foysters have commented that their relationship seemed to be that of father and daughter rather than husband and wife; they were also very attached to each other. Foyster made no attempt to curb his wife's behaviour and she never abandoned him, not even later when he was bedridden and incontinent. To quote another source, '... there remained, as there always had been, a deep affection between Marianne and Lionel Foyster, although this appeared at times to be the relationship of father and daughter, rather than that of husband and wife'.

Their relationship probably developed in an atmosphere of sexually charged fantasy which caused Foyster, in his religious frame of mind, great guilt and anguish. Foyster probably derived vicarious sexual satisfaction from his wife's sexual relationships with other men, and may well have been a voyeur. We must remember that he lived in the same house as Marianne and the bigamous husband, Fisher, and that he tolerated d'Arles at Borley. This vicarious satisfaction was probably the sum of Foyster's sexual activity; his illness prevented him from doing much else after the early 1930s. Thus the long-suffering or deluded husband vanishes, to be replaced by a pervert who was also a sin-obsessed clergyman.

From Marianne's point of view, her marriage with Foyster provided her with emotional security; she was just a 'naughty girl' when she misbehaved; the relationship with Foyster not only gave her an ideal base from which to prosecute her relationships and satisfy her sexual appetite, but also provided her with the cooperation and assistance of a man of some professional and social standing.

The Foysters made a terrible mistake with d'Arles. They probably thought that a street flower-seller would be easy prey and no match for them, but they were wrong. D'Arles was a vicious, cruel man who, it is said, 'was huge sexually'. He lorded it over the frail Rector and dominated the household. He is alleged to have tried to blackmail the Foysters at a later stage.

Another reason for taking on men like d'Arles and Fisher was their poor financial circumstances. Foyster, as we have noted, had lost a considerable sum of money in the Wall Street crash. D'Arles assisted them with the flower-shop project in Wimbledon, and Fisher's father later provided money for a house to be built in Ipswich. D'Arles, however, was a tough customer, who exploited and frightened them. He has been described as 'Rasputin', 'a thoroughly evil man' and 'an extraordinary person'. It is interesting that in *Fifteen Months in a Haunted House* Foyster gave d'Arles the pseudonym 'Mr Lawless'.

*

Now we must consider how the poltergeists fitted into all this. Once the story of the domestic arrangements at the Rectory has been told, the ghosts seem of little importance; yet the alleged poltergeist effects, which were no more than cruel tricks played upon one another by the members of a household which lived in an atmosphere of obsessive love, sexual jealousy and suspicion, reveal even more about the relationships between these extraordinary people.

Foyster began his *Diary of Occurrences at Borley Rectory* as follows:

Since I have been asked by members of our family to tell what I know of the so-called Borley ghost, and since I think it desirable that a record of our experiences should be preserved, I am writing this before the details have gone out of my mind. I should like to say first of all that if I had been told by anyone what I am about to relate, I certainly should not have believed it, unless I had the very highest regard for their general strict adherence to the truth. In fact I have during these last two weeks or so, wondered more than once if I should not presently wake up and find it all a dream; I regret to say that I have not done so yet. Again as far as imagination goes; one can imagine, one has seen things or heard things, or felt things, but one cannot imagine stones and bricks and pictures lying on the floor and things flying about the room and a broken window when these things are still in evidence the next day and the next week.

To begin then. We had, before we came here, heard about my predecessor's experience, and were rather inclined to attribute it to his imagination or to practical jokes played upon him. When we came to Borley first of all, we looked at the Rectory and another possible house, and decided to live in the former, neither of us feeling that there was a particularly uncanny or ghostly atmosphere about it and treating the whole matter, as so many others have done, as practical nonsense.

We came into residence on October 16th, 1930. Our first experience of anything at all out of the way was one which generally one would have naturally forgotten. I was quite tired one evening and was lying down upstairs, when Marianne who was sitting in a room downstairs, came running out to ask if anything was the matter, as she had distinctly heard me call 'Marianne dear' more than once. I had not called at all ...

The reader will note that it was *Marianne* and *not* Foyster himself who heard the voice. That Marianne heard voices, or beheld apparitions, or actually witnessed the movement, appearance or disappearance of objects when no one was near is a consistent feature of Foyster's accounts. The Rector himself appears in the role of a wondering observer, surveying the aftermath of the ghosts' work, and as his wife's amanuensis. Many of the spectacular Borley stunts rely on the uncorroborated testimony of Marianne, or of Edwin Whitehouse, who will be introduced shortly.

After these auditory effects, which included stealthy footsteps
– not something which required a supernatural explanation in a
household such as the Foysters', one would have thought –
Marianne claimed to see apparitions; and not of the nun, but of
Harry Bull, the King Charles's Head of Borley who owed his
ghostly existence to the spite of his sisters, the Misses Bull, and
to their belief (or hope) that he had made a will in their favour
which his widow had somehow supressed. For what do we read
in Foyster's account?

> I cannot remember the exact date, but we had not been in
> the house very long before Marianne began seeing Harry
> Bull ... twice she was with me when she saw him, but I saw
> nothing, which is not to be wondered at, since I am not
> clairvoyant, while she comes from a psychic family ... the
> last time she saw him was some time before Christmas ...
> he seemed generally to be carrying something, *so possibly*
> *he wanted to communicate with her about his will, about*
> *which he might well be uneasy, since it is said that he talked*
> *about making another and possibly did so and it has been*
> *mislaid.* Anyhow, I must not wander into conjecture. [My
> italics]

Here is the tittle-tattle of the Misses Bull coming through,
loud and clear. Marianne was making use not of the nun legend,
but of the story of the possible murder by his wife of Harry Bull
and the alleged suppression of a will in his sisters' favour.

Other events recorded by the marvelling Foyster during the
early stages of the supposed haunting are wonderful only in that
Foyster seems to believe that they require a supernatural
explanation. For example:

> Again an odd smell of cooking would often come through
> our bedroom window between 11 and 12 p.m. Also some of
> our crockery would soon disappear out of the kitchen in a
> wonderful way and presently appear again ... a book was
> left on the windowsill of the W.C. ... I thought it looked
> untidy and took it away. The next day another appeared.

Marianne thereupon expostulated with me about it and then we discovered that neither of us had taken it there ... Marianne missed the milk jug belonging to our breakfast set and some other jugs recently. She said she had looked for them and a tea-pot everywhere and could not find them, and added 'I wish they would bring them back' ... Thursday 26th started with our finding two books had been placed under our bed during the night. Then the bells started ringing.

The bells to which Foyster referred where the house bells, used to summon the servants, not those in his own belfry. Sudden and strident ringing of the bells was another feature of the Borley haunting.

To continue, with what I personally regard as Foyster's *pièce de résistance*:

But on this day, first the front door bell rang with no one there, and then two or three other bells. During the afternoon a whole lot of books were deposited on the rack for warming plates over the kitchen range; these included a number of Durham Mission Hymn Books which we use at the Lent week day services and of which we were rather short, so they were a welcome addition, some rather decrepit A & Ms and two other large books.

Clearly sceptics will throw in the towel after reading this and admit the reality of supernatural intervention in human affairs. This was no doubt all jolly good fun, but things began to take a nasty turn – indeed they became violent and dangerous – in the early spring of 1931, six months after the Foysters had moved into the Rectory. On the evening of the day upon which the miraculous draught of hymn books appeared on the kitchen range (a miracle that surely rivals those of minor Christian saints) Marianne was hurt.

So far it was just amusing, but what followed was not. That night just as we were going to bed, I was in the bathroom and Marianne was on the landing outside our room with a candle in her hand, when suddenly she was hit a terrific blow in the eye which almost stunned her, gave her a cut under the eye, which was bleeding when she got to me in the bathroom and gave her a black eye for some days. She was not near enough to the wall to have collided with it.

On the next night, 27 February:

We had just got to bed and the light was out, when things started flying round the room. First something hit the wall and fell on the bed, which turned out to be a large cotton reel that was standing on the mantel piece [sic] when we went to bed, and then something whizzed fairly close to Marianne's head and fell to the ground with a great clatter. I lit a lamp and discovered the head of a hammer with the broken handle in it lying on the floor.

In spite of the increasing violence of the 'phenomena', Foyster's account loses none of its unintentional humour. For example, we learn that on 28 February 1931 Foyster not only discovered a pin on his chair, with the point upwards, but also that:

Not very long afterwards an erection was discovered outside the door of my study over which I might have fallen if baby had not come along first to say goodnight. It consisted of part of an old lamp and an ancient saucepan, neither of which M. says she has seen before. A little later Marianne came to tell me supper would soon be ready; when I came after a few minutes the long handle of a floor polisher had been put across a door I had to go through though it was not there when M. had passed the door just before.

By this time the reader will have noticed two salient features of Foyster's account. The first is that many of the phenomena seem to be childish pranks. Secondly, if they are more serious than this, such as the blow to Marianne's face when she was out on the landing with a candle, the details rely on Marianne's uncorroborated testimony. The adventure of the floor polisher handle (above) indicates that Marianne was playing tricks on her doddery husband.

By early March, fantastic pantomimes were being acted out at the Rectory. On 9 March:

I do not think I have ever found it quite so hard to go to bed as I did that night. They were generally especially venomous on our way up to bed or just after we got into bed, and their having been so bad during the day, we did not know what to expect at night. Besides that it was getting rather badly on our nerves, and I was wondering how much more we could stand.

At about 10 o'clock I asked M. whether she could stand to stay in the house all night, or should we turn tail and seek asylum at the Bigg's [*sic*]. This though would have meant telling them about the trouble, which we are most anxious to keep to ourselves, also being suspected of incipient insanity. Besides she felt that if she once gave way and ran, she would never be able to face the house again; so after a moment's hesitation she said that she could stand it if I could, so we decided to see it out. Personally, I can say that I never could have done it, if it had not been for my faith in a Higher Power, and I am sure it was the same for Marianne ...

Since things are thrown as a rule from behind us, one of us looked one way and the other going along backwards. At the foot of the stairs M. somewhat collapsed for a time, but we at last got up to the bathroom and then to our bedroom without any demonstration. We kept a light burning in our room, and I did not get to sleep till after 3 a.m. ...

I woke soon after 5; Marianne was awake and showed me a heap of four or five stones that had been piled behind her pillow ...

We note that Foyster states that objects were usually thrown from *behind* him. In fact this was always the case. Marianne, significantly, was the witness of inexplicable movements; all her husband ever saw was objects whizzing past him. Obviously (but not to Foyster) they were thrown by his wife.

The 'phenomena' increased in violence and frequency throughout the spring. Foyster called in various relatives, including Ally Bull, the late Rev. Harry's brother, a number of local parish priests of his acquaintance including the Rev. A.H. Sellwood of Great Cornard, for assistance, and got in touch with the Bishop of Chelmsford. Exorcisms of various sorts were performed, though without any success. Foyster hit on the idea of fumigating the house with creosote when incense was not available, which gave him temporary relief.

In March 1931 – I have not been able to find out the exact date – François junior came into residence. This meant that d'Arles himself was a frequent visitor to Borley. I have already explained that d'Arles was, or soon became, by her own admission, Marianne's lover. Foyster's writings make clear not only that he was often at Borley, but that he often slept in the Rectory itself, although he was supposed to be renting the Rectory cottage. Another interesting revelation in his diaries is that he knew that d'Arles's real name was Pearless. Marianne's son, Ian, claimed that the name 'd'Arles' was used to fool the ever-credulous Foyster about the sort of man he was letting into his household. François d'Arles, it was claimed, was a French-Canadian who had been in the French Secret Service during the First World War.

Even if this is true, Foyster clearly learned early on what his name real was, and this intelligence obviously did not perturb him unduly, for Pearless went on visiting Borley. Again, the traditional sceptic's story of the trusting and credulous Rector, who was imposed upon and deceived in the most fantastic manner by his devious wife, simply will not do. Marianne and Foyster probably colluded in attracting Pearless to Borley; their motives were financial and sexual. The stories about Pearless's exotic antecedents and distinguished wartime career would have been made up not for Foyster, but for the neighbours.

Foyster's *Diary* elaborates on more of the wonders described briefly in his *Summary*:

That evening while we were having our evening meal suddenly a piece of brick fell right on the table close by my plate. If it had gone an inch or so to the right it would have broken something; as it was it just fitted in. *Marianne had risen from the table at the moment and had her back turned and neither of us saw from which direction it came* ... [My italics] The next morning when Marianne went into the kitchen, she found the table on its back with its legs sticking into the air, and the contents of the store cupboard scattered all over the place ... When they start, I tell them aloud in the Name of Christ to go out of the house and not to come back ... A new thing they have started to do, though, is to produce horrible odours, particularly, I think almost exclusively, in my study ... Marianne has been hurt quite badly four times, but never when wearing her scapula. Twice she neglected or forgot putting them on, and once they were on a few minutes before, but the fastening on which she had them round her neck was mysteriously broken.

By this stage of the haunting Foyster felt that enough information was available for him to reach the following conclusion:

There are evidently two quite distinct sets of spirits; – the one very inimical and the other friendly.

The friendly spirits were clearly responsible for the introduction into the Rectory of the following items:

A very useful small tin trunk was discovered in the kitchen; a powder bowl, very much like the one I was going to get M. for Christmas, in the bath room. (She saw it in a shop and was most anxious to have it, but while I was buying other things, someone else bought it, and they had not another.)

In the spring another celebrated feature of the Borley 'haunt' began – the mysterious written messages:

Another strange occurrence is that Marianne's name was at one time continually being written on little odd pieces of paper in a rather shaky childish hand (Adelaide, needless to say, cannot write yet).

Later this was to develop into the writing on the walls, which many Borley investigators have attributed to the ghost of the murdered nun appealing for help from beyond the grave. We note that many of the 'phenomena' are childish tricks, and surely resemble the pranks of a naughty and rather malicious child, trying both to annoy and to attract the attention of its parents. Pins are left on chairs, small objects hit people, furniture is overturned and the contents of cupboards are thrown about. Then we have Marianne's name written in childish script, left on scraps of paper that seem to have been scattered through the house.

Although Marianne later denied that she haunted Borley (and blamed just about everyone else, including her husband), the above incidents do suggest that it was she who initiated the 'haunting' with her stories about voices and apparitions. This needs no further explanation than her propensity to fantasise and the fact that she was a pathological liar. She also loved drawing attention to herself and being the centre of attention. She was always flamboyant and given to exaggerated, theatrical gestures. When she was landed at Borley, which was remote and boring, she obviously found the temptation to exploit the situation irresistible. That she claimed to have seen the ghost of Harry Bull and not the nun is consistent with this; the nun had after all been seen before, and her appearance was not likely to cause great excitement among the Bulls. The appearance of the dead Harry Bull trying to sort out his will, a story that concurs exactly with the malicious gossip being spread by the Misses Bull, was a different matter. This probably explains the early part of the haunting.

I have already discussed the theory that the relationship between Foyster and Marianne developed when she was a little girl, and that it continued, perhaps, through shared fantasies that over a period of time developed an explicitly sexual component. If indeed the Foysters' relationship remained one between adult and child, the childish tricks – most of which seem designed to attract the wonder and attention of Foyster – are readily explained. They were just that, childish tricks, attention-seeking behaviour familiar to some degree to any parents, as familiar as children writing their names on bits of paper and leaving them scattered about the house; Foyster's 'naughty girl' was at it again.

The situation is complicated because not only Marianne was playing ghosts. Village boys – perhaps men and women too – played tricks at the 'haunted' Rectory. According to Ian, who lived at Borley for a short time in early 1933, one village boy named Willy Palmer was actually Marianne's confederate in faking ghostly effects; he rigged up a collapsing shelf in the pantry which at the tug of a string deposited pots and pans on the floor with a great clatter, no doubt to Foyster's wonder.

A further complication is Foyster's declining mental health. His memory was appalling, and according to Marianne he would put things down, promptly forget where they were, and then herald their appearance where he himself had left them with amazement and awe; this presumably explains incidents such as the following:

> Then another really bad bout started on Monday, April 27th. That afternoon Marianne was getting the tea ready, when I noticed a milk jug that I thought I had seen full a few minutes before, quite empty. I asked if it had not had some milk in it, and she said that it had. This was not the first time that a milk jug has mysteriously been emptied. I remarked that we would have a clean jug and not fill that one up again, as I would rather drink after the cat than after those beastly things. Soon afterwards we sat down to tea and things began to fly ...

No doubt Marianne derived some amusement from her husband's wondering greatly at the emptying of jugs, and, like a child, tested him to see how far she could go.

The next really bad day was Saturday (May 2). There was a nasty feeling about the house that evening, which both Marianne and myself noted. We were sitting in the kitchen as it was chilly and we had no other fire in the house, and we could hear weird sounds from the front part of the house before the storm actually broke. Then it suddenly started and we had the worst half-hour that we have ever had. We were having a late evening meal and Marianne was cooking some things for it, when things started flying about the kitchen and Marianne had pepper thrown in her eyes. We sat down to our meal and tried to take no notice, but it was very nerve racking never knowing at what moment there was going to be a bang or where a stone or some other implement was going to land. Amongst other things thrown, a table knife hit me on the hand. We felt we would have to do something and we were lamenting that I had not sent for any incense, when we thought of some creosote we had in the house. I went to get it and Marianne came after me. I was hit on the neck by a great piece of hard mortar on the way there and a spanner touched my hair on the way back. However, as soon as we got the creosote burning, we smoked them out and everything quietened down at once. I went with it through the house, but not into any of the rooms. I certainly should have gone into our bedroom, but foolishly did not think of it. We paid for this omission, for we had settled down for the night when pepper was dropped on to our faces. This was a second dose for Marianne.

Marianne has denied that she ever faked 'phenomena'. But when Price and his team visited Borley in October 1931, they at once, as has already been related, suspected her. According to Mrs K.M. Goldney, the Secretary of the Society for Psychical research, who was present, when Marianne realised that she was under suspicion she fell to her knees and implored St Anthony for vindication by allowing a poltergeist effect to be demonstrated to her visitors. She was rewarded with the ringing of a bell.

Marianne also accused Foyster of playing at ghosts. She

claims that she once watched the Rector strewing ashes from the hall stove about the floor, and that later he claimed that 'The Things' were responsible. Ian held Foyster blameless but accused Marianne and her lover, d'Arles, of deliberately persecuting the ailing Rector. If this was the case, their actions were cruel, for his physical and mental health were rapidly declining.

That Marianne was responsible for the initial phase of the haunting is indisputable. Foyster's attitude to the flying hammers and clouds of pepper is more problematical. Undoubtedly he was an easy man to impose upon because of his forgetfulness; but his lapses of memory can explain only minor events, empty milk jugs, the appearance of pots of tea, the miraculous powder bowls and so on. Ian related that Marianne exploited her husband's failing memory in a number of ways. Foyster was always careful with money to the point of meanness, and she circumvented his parsimony with ingenious subterfuges. For example, when she saw a dress she greatly admired but which they could not afford she purchased material of a similar pattern and made an ostentatious start on sewing it herself. Then she put the sewing on one side and, after a decent interval, bought the dress anyway. On another occasion she bought a powder bowl that she wanted but could not afford, and introduced this to the Rectory as what psychical researchers call an 'apport'. Presumably the tin travelling trunk that appeared in the kitchen, to Foyster's consternation, had a similar origin.

The problem is that Foyster must, at an early stage, have realised that tricks were being played on him. What was his reaction to this discovery? He did not, it seems, remonstrate with his naughty child-wife but went on recording the 'phenomena', regaling his family with accounts of his supernatural experiences in the 'family circular' and publicly defending Marianne against all sceptics. Why?

According to Marianne, Foyster was very worried about how they would manage after his retirement, which, because of his poor health, could not be long delayed. The solution they eventually came up with was a bigamous marriage in which Foyster pretended to be his wife's father; but at this stage, Foyster must have been very worried about his finances. The Foysters' involvement with d'Arles, not only in a sexual context, but in connection with the projected florist's business in London, has already been mentioned. Foyster had the idea of writing a bestselling thriller, and was therefore prepared to go along with the Borley escapades, and to defend his wife publicly, even though he too knew she was a fraud. If he had such ambitions, this would account for his anger at the opinion expressed by Price during his visit, and for his unsympathetic attitude to Price for some years afterwards. For example, when Foyster heard that Price intended to talk about Borley at a public lecture, he threatened him with legal action.

Foyster worked on his novel (or thriller) for years. The result was *Fifteen Months in a Haunted House*, a rambling, rather incoherent and thinly veiled version of his diaries. It was never published; Harry Price wrote the sensational books about Borley. But during the period of the alleged haunting Foyster no doubt hoped to repair his fortunes by writing a sensational and bestselling book under an alias. The reader will remember that Price wasn't the first person to have this idea, for it had already occurred to the Smiths.

This theory also accounts for Foyster's experimenting with poltergeist effects and the reaction of those who observe them, by strewing ashes from the stove over the hall floor and then blaming 'The Things'. This was probably not an isolated incident. What it does not account for are the activities of M. François d'Arles, who also played at ghosts and appears to have persecuted the old Rector.

That Marianne and d'Arles were lovers is beyond doubt. Their relationship was, from Marianne's own account, devoid of any affection and revolved around mutual sexual satisfaction. It was also mutually exploitative in other ways. D'Arles was always said to be 'snooping' round the Rectory. Several years later he tried to blackmail them by threatening to expose Foyster's domestic arrangements to the Bishop of Chelmsford. The Foysters no doubt thought that they could exploit d'Arles, using him to run the florist's business in Wimbledon. D'Arles, though not in love with Marianne, may also have wanted to possess her more completely than he was able to while the strange triangular relationship persisted. It is important to understand that at no stage did Marianne give the slightest hint that she wanted to leave Foyster. What a strange situation it must have been for this 'sexually huge' man, this 'Rasputin' of the Rectory, to be called in as a kind of stud to satisfy the wife of a man who none the less enjoyed a relationship with his spouse with which he, d'Arles, could not compete.

Given that by nature d'Arles was vicious and dishonest, one does not have to look much further for other sources of rancour. The feeble, crippled husband unable to satisfy his wife was d'Arles's social superior, for he was a Cambridge-educated cleric, of the Foysters of Hastings and the grand Tillards of Stukely Hall. No wonder d'Arles is said to have gloated over the old Rector, and to have made his life miserable by playing his own ghostly tricks in the house.

So it is that the fog of poltergeists and ghosts dissolves, and we see the cruel and malicious tricks played upon one another by the members of a household who lived in an atmosphere of mutual suspicion, sexual jealousy and obsessive love.

9

The Writing on the Wall

The haunting developed through the late spring and summer of 1931, and more and more outsiders were drawn into the charade, a process which culminated in the visit of Harry Price in October. Apart from the usual catalogue of 'phenomena', faithfully recorded by Foyster for a grateful posterity, certain other features of the later haunting are worth mentioning, again because of the light they shed upon the workings of the Borley household. It is in the summer of 1931 that Edwin Whitehouse makes his ill-fated appearance on the stage.

Sir George and Lady Whitehouse lived at Arthur Hall, a country house just off the main road running between Sudbury and Long Melford, which is now an Italian restaurant. Arthur Hall is not far from Borley, and Sir George was a churchwarden there; both he and his wife were frequent visitors to the Rectory and had witnessed some of its wonders, including a fire that had started in the skirting boards of a locked room. On 6 June their nephew, Edwin, arrived at their house for a holiday during which he hoped to recuperate from a nervous breakdown. He could hardly have chosen a worse place.

Edwin Whitehouse is almost as enigmatic a figure as Foyster or Marianne. He later became a Benedictine monk at St Augustine's Abbey, Ramsgate, but continued to suffer from chronic depression and mental breakdowns. I was told by a member of the community at Ramsgate that Edwin – or Dom Richard as he became – had suffered terrible experiences at the Battle of Jutland, and that these were responsible for his subsequent mental instability.

His later experiences at Borley certainly didn't help. Marianne described him as follows:

> Edwin was usually praying and wanted everyone to join him, or expounding theory. He wasn't sure whether he wanted to be a Spiritualist or a Roman Catholic. He did, however, become a Roman Catholic.

Now we turn again to Foyster's *Diary*:

> Another thing I should mention. I believe that I stated in my first account that the word 'Marianne' was at one time often found written on scraps of paper; Lady W. suggested that we should write 'What do you want?' underneath one of these, which I did. The next day there appeared what I read as 'Rest', but which Marianne declared is 'Pest' (it might be either, I think) underneath, while on another paper appeared 'Marianne help me'. I wrote 'How?' underneath that, but no answer has been given.

This part of Foyster's *Diary* takes us up to 7 May 1931. He continued his *Diary* with ' "Borley Ghost". Third Instalment' as follows:

> I finished my second instalment about May 11th, 1931 and I now carry on my account from then. We had a very quiet time for some weeks; now and then something or other was thrown, but we at once burned incense and there was nothing more, so we really began to feel we knew how to get any trouble stopped. *During this time there was some very mysterious writing on the walls* [My italics]. I mentioned writing on papers before. 'Marianne' appeared one day on the wall of the passage leading to the bathroom. It looked as if the writer had been pulled away just while he was finishing, since the end of the 'e' went up in the air and the 'i' was not dotted. I wrote underneath it 'What can we do?' but no notice was taken of it. Later a little further along the

Borley 'wall writing' (above), with Marianne's signature for comparison (below).

passage was written 'Marianne please get help' and then a dash as if again someone had been pulled away. Later still further along the passage was written 'Marianne get help (something indecipherable) bother me' or bothers me. Marianne wrote underneath 'I cannot understand, tell me more. Marianne.' Something was then added underneath but subsequently written over.

Then, at about the time young Whitehouse (who was about the same age as Marianne) appeared, the messages took on a distinctly Roman Catholic tone. Marianne had long been flirting with Roman Catholicism, and used to attend Mass at the Catholic Church in Sudbury and return to Borley and attend church there, much to the embarrassment of her husband. A maid who lived in the Rectory during 1932, and whose account of what she observed will be given in detail later, claimed that

Marianne – who as far as can be discovered was never formally received into the Roman church – attempted to convert her to the Roman faith. Whitehouse, it will be remembered, was deeply interested in both Spiritualism and Roman Catholicism.

Foyster wrote:

> Some time later, was written one day while we were in the house, 'Get light mass and prayers here'. When we first saw it, the 'here' was not written and then a short time afterwards we found it added … On Saturday evening, June 6th, Lady Whitehouse brought up a nephew of hers who was very much interested in Poltergeistism, also her son to see what there was to be seen and naturally there was a lot of talk in the house on the subject.

Foyster's account of the wall writings is curious. While he is careful to give dates, and to try to keep an approximately chronological record of startling events, such as the appearance of the Durham Mission hymn books on the kitchen warming rack, he is vague about the scribblings on the wall. Indeed he omits to mention those that appeared in June in his *Summary of Experiences*; yet, if the testimony of Whitehouse, who became a Borley enthusiast and contributed his own accounts of the haunting to the Borley literature, is taken at face value, the wall writings that appeared in June, after his arrival, are among the most spectacular of the many 'phenomena'.

June was a noisy and violent month at the Rectory, and things came to such a pass that the Foysters temporarily moved out and went to stay at Arthur Hall with the Whitehouses. No doubt Marianne found this sojourn in a country house very agreeable; and young Edwin, who was fascinated by the haunting, accompanied Marianne on walks to the Rectory every day for nine days, not only to see what was happening there, but also to make a Novena to ask for special guidance. They would pray and recite the rosary together in the empty house.

During one of these visits, according to Whitehouse's own memoir:

The Novena over, Mrs Foyster walked back towards the Blue Room to investigate, and I thought I would look at the walls downstairs. I returned a couple of minutes later and Mrs Foyster joined me on the landing. We compared notes, but neither of us had anything to report. Happening to turn my eyes towards a bit of wall that jutted out from the landing, a point directly opposite where we had been kneeling, I was surprised to notice a fresh bit of writing on an otherwise clean bit of wall.

The message that had appeared was one of those distinctively Roman Catholic ones. It read: 'Get light mass and prayers.' The fact that Whitehouse was downstairs, while Marianne had remained upstairs, when the famous message appeared indicates – as most reasonable people would in any case conclude – that Marianne was responsible. Marianne had been amusing herself with childish messages for some time, but the reason for the abrupt change of style to requests for masses seems obvious; these were written to maintain and quicken the interest of Edwin Whitehouse, upon whom Marianne had designs.

Whitehouse extended his stay at Arthur Hall into the winter of 1931 and spent a great deal of time with the Foysters. Whether she succeeded in seducing him is impossible to say, but it is not unreasonable to suppose that she planned, or attempted, to do so. Marianne had an unpleasant habit of preying upon mentally unstable men; the story of her bigamous marriage to the commercial traveller, and her treatment of a bereaved doctor, which will be related in their place, illustrate this. Whitehouse was going through a bad time; he was recuperating from a breakdown, and in fact suffered further relapses. The strain imposed upon him by the temptation that Marianne was offering, when he was an obsessively religious, disturbed man, deeply interested in the occult and contemplating entry into a celibate priesthood, must have been intolerable. Marianne could be very cruel, and with Whitehouse, as with many other men, she seems to have acted with a complete disregard for his feelings and well-being.

Whitehouse became an ardent supporter of Marianne against her detractors who accused her of faking the Borley wonders, and he mounted his own campaign of vindication, even seeking out the Smiths to interview them about their experiences at Borley. He also contributed his own testimony to Price's books, claiming that while in Marianne's company, in the Rectory kitchen, and in her bedroom while she was suffering from one of her periodic illnesses (marked by fatigue and a headache), he witnessed the most spectacular poltergeist effects. Whitehouse is always cited by the Borley cultists as one of the most impressive and convincing witnesses. For her part Marianne denies not only that she ever had designs on him but that he ever saw any poltergeists at the Rectory.

According to Trevor Hall, who interviewed Whitehouse's aunt in the 1950s, Lady Whitehouse maintained that Marianne was 'man mad', that Borley 'did Edwin no good at all' and that eventually Whitehouse's father forbade him to visit the Rectory. In late 1931 Edwin left the district and suffered another breakdown.

Whitehouse stuck to his account of what had happened throughout his life. The Abbot of Ramsgate would not allow me to interview the members of his community who still remember Edwin (or 'Dom Richard'), and accused me of wishing to calumniate the dead. The irony of this, of course, is that calumny of the dead was what Whitehouse himself was perpetrating by supporting the theory that a member of the Waldegrave family had murdered a French nun whom he had made his mistress. I did, however, manage to speak on the phone to a member of the community who told me that Dom Richard became very angry when the Society for Psychical Research Report on Borley was mentioned; this was because the authors had suggested that his mental and emotional problems might be relevant when considering the worth of his testimony. Let us hope that the Abbot is not one of those religious who wax eloquent about the growth of pseudo-religious cults and the occult.

Whitehouse was ordained in 1940 and died in the late 1970s. A curious feature of Foyster's novel based on Borley is the character he invented for Whitehouse. Whitehouse became Miss

Edith Graycastle, the *niece* of Sir Robert and Lady Greycastle of Laburnham Hall.

The Borley wall writings were later to play an important part in the development of the theories about the origins of the ghosts. The nun was revived, and it was alleged that it was she, from beyond the grave, who was pencilling the pathetic appeals on the walls.

*

Apart from the usual catalogue of events, and the continuing involvement of Edwin Whitehouse with the Foysters, the most significant events of late 1931 were, first, the visit of a medium, who had come to sort out the ghosts, and secondly, the visit of Harry Price in October; this was to have momentous consequences for Marianne, as we shall see – the publicity that Price gave to Borley ten years later was to make her a target for every psychical researcher, and would lead to the appearance of a private detective at her door in the snowy wastes of North Dakota.

The visit of the medium is quite amusing as related by Foyster in his awful novel. In this work Foyster calls himself John Fowler and his wife Emily Jane. It is in the following passage that he uses the significant name 'Teed' as a pseudonym for the medium's assistant:

So the day arrived, and the hour – 6 p.m., and the company. Mr Buttle introduced his two companions, Mr Thompson, the medium, and Mr Teed, the interrogator. First of all they looked round the house and remarked that it had a haunted atmosphere. Then they decided that they would like to sit in the library. Not only was I allowed in, but I was pressed into service. Mr Buttle and myself had to sit in the circle with the two chief actors. Emily Jane was for the time being engaged elsewhere.

For the sake of anyone who is unfamiliar with what takes place at a 'sitting', I will explain that the medium goes into a trance; while in this condition it is claimed that his spirit

vacates his body which is then temporarily inhabited by
another spirit, who acts and speaks through the body it is
possessing. It was Teed's part to draw out information from
the spirit in possession.

We sat down and Mr Thompson soon flew into a trance.
Then he began to talk.

'This is his Guide on the other side,' I was told (a sort of
chucker out); 'he is an Indian.'

Very soon his manner changed. 'This is his Guide; a
doctor.' He shook hands all round, and when he came to me
he asked me if I was not troubled with rheumatism? I
admitted that I was, so he gave me general directions on the
subject of food.

The proceedings were all Greek to me, but – here he was
changing again.

The Interrogator got interested.

'Give me a drink,' cried the Medium, or rather the spirit in
possession.

'My friend, you could not drink if I did,' replied Teed.

'Give me a drink,' the spirit still persisted.

'Friend, you have no body to put it into; it –'

'Give me a drink, I say.'

'Who are you, friend; what is your name?'

'My name? Why, Joe Miles to be sure.'

'And what is your occupation?'

'Occupation?'

'Yes, what do you do for a living?'

'I keep a public house, and I want a drink.'

'Are you aware that your body is dead and buried; it is only
your spirit speaking to us?'

Foyster (as John Fowler) explains that Joe Miles, the thirsty
spirit, was enlightened about his transformation from corrup-
tible publican to incorruptible spirit, and sent on his way. The
spiritualists promised that Joe Miles had been responsible for
all the trouble at the Rectory, and that the problem was now
solved. Alas, this was not so. In his *Summary of Experiences*,
Foyster commented tersely:

August. A medium and an investigator come down and hold
a seance. Different spirits are tackled, among them Joe
Miles, who, it was declared, was responsible for the
disturbances. However, it appeared subsequently that this
was a mistake.

Brief though the quotation from Foyster's novel is, it is
representative of the whole in both style and content, and one
can only be amazed that Foyster ever entertained serious hopes
for eventual publication.

In January 1932, the Marks Tey Spiritualist Circle visited
Borley in force; they were rather more efficient than Mr Teed
and his medium, and succeeded in laying the ghosts. They were
led by the materialising medium Mr Guy L'Estrange, and
claimed that they had contacted the spirit of the nun; it was she,
after all, and not the bibulous Joe Miles (who had evidently been
trying to make himself heard at the bar) who had been causing
all the trouble. After their visit, the 'phenomena' abruptly
ceased.

By early 1932 the Foysters, both of whom cooperated with the
fraudulent haunting, must have realised that they had gone far
enough. Foyster had enough material for his book and was to
spend the next ten years tinkering with it. They had encouraged
visits by professional investigators and been exposed. Although
the Borley literature makes great play with the testimony of the
Whitehouses, the opinions of other neighbours who knew the
Foysters are ignored; various local worthies had come to the not
very surprising conclusion that Marianne was behind much of
what went on; in particular, Sir John Braithwaite, whose sister,
a JP, lived in nearby Long Melford, expressed the opinion that
Marianne was responsible for the wall writing.

The play-acting and confidence tricks now had to stop, and an
ideal way of doing this was to accept that the Marks Tey
Spiritualist Circle had indeed exorcised the ghosts. It is
interesting that the earlier attempt which took place before
Price's visit was unsuccessful, in spite of the strenuous efforts of
the medium and Mr Teed, and that the exorcism of the Marks
Tey Circle, which happened after Marianne had been accused of

fraud by Price, was successful. The Foysters realised that if they carried on they risked not only their credibility and standing in the community, but could well invite a closer scrutiny of their lives that would bring to light their domestic arrangement with d'Arles, who, it must be remembered, was during this period pleasuring Mrs Foyster. So the ghosts had to leave, and they did. But d'Arles stayed; and although there were no more ghosts, the household at Borley was to surpass itself in eccentricity during the next few years.

10

The Wildgoose, the Greenwood
and the Monk

The reason for the speculation and conjecture about what was going on behind the scenes at Borley during the period of the great haunting is that there was no reliable witness, living in the house, who does not fall under the suspicion of suffering from chronic emotional disturbances. In 1932, however, Marianne employed a nurse-companion, Miss Dytor, who later married and became Mrs Wildgoose. She lived with the Foysters in the Rectory from May to November. Her description of the household, which was ordered much as it had been in 1931 except for the absence of 'The Things', is fascinating. The problem with her story is that although it confirms what has already been tentatively suggested about the relationship between Foyster and Marianne it raises more questions: in particular, the true parentage of the baby who appeared at Borley in the early summer of 1932, and who died there in September. Before considering this problem I shall summarise what she said about the Borley household and the relationship between the three adults, Foyster, Marianne and d'Arles.

Miss Dytor had replied to an advertisement in the *Nursing Mirror* placed by Marianne for a nurse to assist her with caring for a new-born baby. Miss Dytor was under the impression that this child was Marianne's, and when she met her she formed the opinion that she had indeed given birth to a child not long before. This opinion was presumably based upon Marianne's physical condition, though the records of the interviews available to me, which were conducted by Trevor Hall on two occasions, in 1953 and 1956, are unclear about this.

During Miss Dytor's residence, Foyster was in poor health; his hands were swollen and he walked with a limp. D'Arles was in attendance, and though he rented the Rectory cottage, a building only a few yards from the Rectory itself, he took his meals with the Foysters and spent much time with them. But Miss Dytor formed the opinion that Marianne not only disliked d'Arles but was actually frightened of him. She also believed that Foyster resented his presence and was jealous of him. This is interesting, because although Foyster acquiesced in the installation of his wife's lover in his own home the arrangement also caused him some anguish. This is not incompatible with his also deriving some vicarious and voyeuristic pleasure from the situation. He was capable of both tolerating it and 'hollering about sin' from the pulpit.

Foyster was very concerned about household expenditure and would sometimes do the cooking himself, producing unappetising concoctions such as boiled rice and macaroni. Marianne disliked the vast, lonely house and Borley in general, and Foyster relieved the tedium of her existence by shutting himself away in his study to work on *Fifteen Months in a Haunted House*, which Miss Dytor read in manuscript form. The atmosphere at the Rectory was said to be strained and unpleasant, which is hardly surprising.

Miss Dytor was told that d'Arles had answered an advertisement placed in a newspaper by Marianne who wanted a companion for little Adelaide. Again we note that there are conflicting accounts of this episode, for sometimes d'Arles is alleged to have placed the original advertisement, because he was looking for a billet for *his* little boy, François junior, and sometimes Marianne is supposed to have been responsible. Miss Dytor was told that d'Arles was employed in a film studio at Elstree, which he wasn't. Here we remember the other story told of d'Arles's past, that he was a French Canadian who had been in the Secret Service during the First World War. In *Fifteen Months in a Haunted House*, Mr Lawless, the d'Arles figure, is also described as having been a member of the Secret Service. The explanation that these stories were invented for the benefit of Foyster makes no sense; first, if d'Arles's presence at the Rectory was due either to his or to Marianne's response to an advertisement, there was no need for him to appear as anything other than what he was; secondly, according to this story it was François junior (not d'Arles himself) who was to live with the Foysters; so any objections that Foyster might have had to d'Arles because of his lowly background could not have been all that serious. Clearly the involvement of d'Arles with Borley was suspicious from the beginning, and the story of the advertisement – even if one was actually placed in a paper – is a cover for the relationship that already existed between him and Marianne. The other d'Arles stories seem to be a mixture of Marianne's own fantasy – she loved to endow not only herself but her friends and acquaintances with exotic, fictitious backgrounds – and tales that were told to neighbours and visitors to Borley to conceal what was really going on. The Misses Bull believed that d'Arles was employed at Elstree, although they also expressed the opinion that he was 'extraordinary'.

Miss Dytor described d'Arles as a short, dark, stoutish man of about Marianne's age; he had been a street flower-seller in London, and was said to be a very competent floral worker. This gave rise to another money-spinning project by the Foysters, the idea of opening a florist's business; it was being planned and discussed while Miss Dytor was at Borley. By this time the Foysters and d'Arles were so heavily involved with each other that breaking the connection would have been difficult; when the end did come, late in 1934, it was fraught with recriminations and threats of blackmail.

In her 1958 interview with the American investigator Robert Swanson, Marianne had some interesting things to say about her former lover:

Swanson: How soon after he arrived at Borley that [*sic*] you had sexual relations with him?
Marianne: I saw him once, then he went away. It was

during that time that he talked about his child. As I
remember, Lionel said: Well that will be good for Adelaide,
because she was a very quiet and lonely child. D'Arles
brought the boy down one Saturday, leaving him there. He
didn't return for about a month or six weeks – I am not
positive about the time. We became very attached to
François junior. I think that it was several weeks before
we had sexual relations.

Swanson: You felt that you liked him when he first arrived,
right?

Marianne: Not particularly, but I was kind of desperate.

Swanson: You needed sex?

Marianne: Yes.

Swanson: While you were having relations with d'Arles,
Lionel was usually shut in his room because he felt ill, is
that correct?

Marianne: He was always given to much reading; even
though he was very fond of me, he didn't like me disturbing him in there and he certainly didn't like Ian in there
nor Miss Dytor.

Swanson: When you told Lionel that you were sleeping with
d'Arles and he said you were a naughty girl, was he still
friendly with d'Arles?

Marianne: He told d'Arles that he should be ashamed of
himself.

Swanson: But you continued to have relations because you
had to be satisfied?

Marianne: After it was started, I realised that I had made a
mistake – because I didn't really – we fought cats and
dogs, that's true.

Swanson: But it was a sex satisfaction that was the urge
there?

Marianne: Yes.

Later in the same interview, Marianne made the following
statement about d'Arles:

It was a very stormy relationship. He was a very dictatorial
man.

That the relationship was stormy no doubt accounts for the occasional appearance of members of the Borley household at the breakfast table sporting black eyes, a 'phenomenon' that many trained and serious investigators have attributed to attacks by spectres. D'Arles himself claimed to have had a fight with a ghost in the kitchen passage, and a ghost was supposed to have struck Adelaide across the face.

*

Miss Dytor also claimed that while she was at Borley Marianne received expensive presents from a man in London, who, she was told, was an old family friend from their Canadian days. He was named Santiago Monk, a diplomat at the Chilean Embassy; he was listed as Commercial Attaché until 1939, when his name vanished from the diplomatic list. Marianne not only referred to Santiago Monk as her 'spiritual godfather' but was later to weave him into one of her fantastic tales about her grand antecedents, claiming that she was really Marianne Monk, the daughter of the incredible Santiago by a lady modestly described as the Countess Sarah Von Kiergraff, late of Schleswig-Holstein. The circumstances of this imposture, and its consequences, will be dealt with later. Marianne has vigorously denied that she had an affair with Santiago, or that she received presents from him. She did, however, make trips up to London to see her 'spiritual godfather'.

We must now consider the origins of the mysterious baby at Borley who had provided the reason for Miss Dytor's employment. She not only was given to understand that the baby was Marianne's – and therefore by implication Foyster's – but was convinced, on the basis of her professional experience, that Marianne had given birth in the early part of 1932. Again, there are a host of conflicting stories. D'Arles, according to Ian, who was to appear at Borley in 1933, was convinced that the child was his. Ian said that he himself saw d'Arles praying at the baby's unmarked grave in Borley churchyard. Miss Dytor related how both Marianne *and* d'Arles were very grieved when the baby died, and that both spent much time weaving floral

garlands to place upon its grave. Yet Marianne later claimed
that the child, John, was adopted. Who was he?

The registers at Borley contain the following entry:

John Evemond Emery. Adopted child of the Reverend L.A.
and Mrs Foyster. Aged 4½ months. Buried in Borley
churchyard, September 12, 1932.

This date must be incorrect, because the child's death was
registered according to the law, and the death certificate states
that a John Evemond Emery died on 20 September 1932 at
Borley Rectory in Essex. The causes of death were convulsions
and marasmas. Marianne Foyster reported the death.

Trevor Hall searched for the birth certificate and found that
the only possible candidate was a John (no Evemond) Emery
born on 25 April 1932 at 30 Swanage Road, Southend-on-Sea,
Essex. He also discovered that this had been the address of a
midwife. The space on the certificate for the father's name was
blank, indicating that the birth had been illegitimate. The
mother, however, although not named Foyster, had exactly the
same initials as Marianne – M.E.R. Her home address was in
Kent.

Marianne had a habit of adopting children throughout her
life. The most obvious explanation, that she did adopt the child
of an unmarried mother from, as she claims, a London adoption
agency, is therefore probably correct. Yet there is the
professional judgment of Miss Dytor about her physical
condition. Furthermore, Marianne was away from Borley in the
early spring, allegedly 'resting' from her unpleasant experiences
with the ghosts.

As we shall see, Marianne was later to adopt children and
successfully convince men upon whom she had designs and with
whom she had enjoyed sexual relations that they were the
fathers and she was the mother. She may have played such a
trick on d'Arles. The problem with this explanation is the
motive. In the other cases referred to, which will be described
later, it was quite clear; she was trying to trap them into
marrying her, and she succeeded every time. Obviously she

could not be doing this with d'Arles, who was well-known in the Borley district by this time, and who was aware of her marital status. She may have told d'Arles that the baby was hers and that he was the father for two reasons: first, she appears to have been incapable of telling the truth about even trivial matters and was given to fantasy and romance; secondly, it might have been a cruel trick to pay him back for his domination of and interference in the Borley household.

If the child was really Marianne's, however, there were good reasons for indulging in the elaborate subterfuge of claiming that it was adopted. She was married to a sick man, many years her senior; they had already enjoyed ten years of childless marriage. Friends and relations, who must have entertained some suspicions about the domestic arrangements at the Rectory, would perhaps have drawn the obvious conclusion if Marianne had suddenly announced that she was pregnant.

Given the length of time that has elapsed since the events, there seems no way of settling this question. It is interesting because of Marianne's later habit of adopting children. The most reasonable explanation of the unfortunate little John Evemond Emery's brief existence is that he was an illegitimate baby whom Marianne adopted.

A further question is why Marianne didn't become pregnant when she indulged in violent sexual activity with several partners. Contraceptives were of course available in the 1930s, but given the spontaneity and apparent ferocity of her liaisons, it is rather surprising that they were successfully applied on every occasion. During the interview in 1958 with Robert Swanson, the following exchange took place:

Swanson: Would you tell me about your sex urge?
Marianne: I used to go for months without any sex at all, then it would come suddenly and sporadically, with a sort of overwhelming vehemence.
Swanson: You had to have someone at that time?
Marianne: Yes.

*

Miss Dytor left Borley in November 1932. In January 1933 Ian returned from Canada and spent three months at the Rectory before moving to Wimbledon with his mother and d'Arles, where they all lived over the flower shop in Worple Road. Ian was a prolific source of information about Marianne, d'Arles and Foyster, and his account of life at Borley provides another vignette of the household. His account broadly agrees with Miss Dytor's; he claimed that he got to know d'Arles well, who imparted the interesting intelligence to the 18-year-old that his mother was a 'sexual maniac', and that the affair between them had started one day when she had persuaded him to take her out in the side-car of his motorcycle for a ride into a lonely part of the country. Marianne complained that she felt unwell, and they stopped in this sequestered spot; the rest, as they say, is history.

D'Arles also said that Marianne was a drug-addict, but she explained that she simply sniffed face-powder from the back of her hand, telling d'Arles that it was cocaine, because she knew it annoyed him. Ian was convinced that his mother had borne d'Arles's child in 1932, but this was based upon d'Arles's own conviction, not on independent information. He confirmed Miss Dytor's observation that d'Arles and Marianne wore similar thick gold wedding bands on their ring fingers; d'Arles explained to Ian that they had been married 'in the sight of God', presumably in that leafy dell they found on their motorcycling expedition.

Ian also made an interesting statement about the ghosts that had plagued Borley. He claimed to have found by accident some string dangling out of the ivy in the wall in the courtyard. When it was tugged it rang some of the house bells, for it was attached to a group of exposed bell-wires. This seems to dispose of the need to invoke the ghost of a strangled nun to 'explain' the 'paranormal' bell ringing.

*

From February 1933 until November 1934 Marianne and d'Arles ran the flower shop in Wimbledon, where they lived as man and wife. Marianne only came home to Borley at weekends, which suggests that the parishioners were prepared to be very tolerant towards their Rector's wife. Marianne befriended a Mr and Mrs Fenton, who owned and ran a nearby chemist's shop, and told them a wonderful tale about her background. This is fascinating, because it gives much insight into the workings of her mind and the material from which she concocted her fantasies. Marianne later admitted that she told her tales as a sort of soap-opera, with herself as the main character, and this is borne out by the following account of herself that she gave to the Fentons.

She had not, of course, been born to an unsuccessful private tutor at Guy Wood Cottages, Romiley, Cheshire; by no means, for she was Marianne Monk before her marriage to d'Arles, Marianne Monk the daughter of Santiago Monk of the Chilean diplomatic service and the magnificent Countess Sarah von Kiergraff – late of Schleswig-Holstein. The real circumstances of her life were woven into her story in a most ingenious and imaginative way. Her diplomat father was, of course, obliged to travel, and because of this Marianne Monk was brought up by a family friend who was none other than that indispensable piece of ecclestiastical furniture, the Reverend Lionel Algernon Foyster, M.A., late of Pembroke College, Cambridge. In spite of this auspicious beginning, Marianne's life had none the less been tragic. For she had gone to Canada with the Rev. Foyster, where he adopted a son. And who was this son? Why, none other than that former luminary of Elstree Studios, that doyen of the French Secret Service during the First World War, M. François d'Arles! Although she fell in love with another, old Mr Foyster always wanted her to marry d'Arles; which Marianne, no doubt shedding a tearful sigh for her true love, dutifully did. And so here they were running the florist's shop in Worple Road, Wimbledon, Mr and Mrs Foyster d'Arles.

Other acquaintances were woven into the tale. For example, she claimed that Sir George and Lady Whitehouse were her cousins, and that she frequently visited them at their grand country seat, Arthur Hall, which visits were occasions of much genteel jocularity and familiarity when she, the former Marianne Monk, called Sir George 'Georgy Porgy dear' in his own ancestral halls. Drawing on the maiden name of Foyster's grandmother, Baumgartner, she claimed to be related to a fictitious Roman Catholic priest, who administered the holy sacraments in Colchester, and who rejoiced in the same name. Drawing inspiration no doubt from her husband's education, Marianne claimed to be a graduate of one of the Cambridge ladies' colleges. She was careful to choose places, people and experience of which her real life had provided her with some knowledge, and for which she could easily provide circumstantial detail. No doubt Foyster was full of Cambridge anecdotes. The Whitehouses and her relatives by marriage, the Bulls, provided her with sufficient material about the English squierarchy. And, of course, there was the dependable Santiago Monk, always ready to be pressed into service in a fantasy.

Mrs Fenton never seems to have doubted the veracity of the tales she was told, and later believed that Marianne had been employed in the British Secret Service during the *Second* World War. The Borley household seems to have been employed in the Secret Service with the same monotonous regularity with which they beheld spectres.

Perhaps the most fantastic part of what Mrs Fenton had to say about the Foysters related to 'old Mr Foyster' himself, who, when he appeared in Wimbledon, and later, when Mrs Fenton visited the Foysters in Suffolk (after Foyster had retired), happily pretended to be his wife's father. He even expressed his satisfaction that Marianne had broken with the brutal d'Arles and found a 'nice chap', Fisher, the mad commercial traveller. This is conclusive evidence for the collusion between Foyster and Marianne that we have discussed before.

The flower shop was closed in November 1934, with threats of blackmail by d'Arles and the intervention of Foyster's lawyer brother, Bernard. D'Arles took himself off to another part of Wimbledon, accompanied by a 16-year-old girl who had been employed in the shop and with whom he is said to have become involved, and set up another business; after this he vanished from the Borley story. Marianne returned to Borley, but remained in touch with the Fentons of Worple Road, often arriving unannounced when she was visiting London. Plate 5 shows Marianne brandishing a bottle of whisky in the back garden of her shop. Plate 6 shows her with Mrs Fenton.

Marianne made an interesting statement about the Fentons when interviewed by Robert Swanson:

Swanson: You stated that you came from an aristocratic family; the daughter of Count and Sarah von Kiergraff of Schleswig-Holstein and that you were with the British Intelligence Service. Explain these untruths.

Marianne: Well, those were flights of fancy; kind of a soap opera. It seems so horribly silly, but it seemed a lot of fun at the time to tell a continuous story. I told her all kinds of silly things and if she'd had sense enough to say shut up and don't tell me fairy tales, it would have been much better.

*

After the failure of the flower shop and her returned to Borley, Marianne embarked upon what is perhaps her most fantastic escapade: the bigamous marriage to a mentally unstable commercial traveller named Henry Francis Fisher (Plate 8), who lived with both Foysters for many years convinced not only that Foyster was his father-in-law, but also that two children whom Marianne obtained from adoption agencies were his own; which is not a great tribute to his mental health.

By late 1934 the Foysters were in very great trouble; Foyster's retirement could not be long delayed, because of his declining health, and they would have to live on a meagre pension of £125 p.a., supplemented by £16 in rents. Their business venture had failed. All Foyster had was his literary aspirations as he worked on *Fifteen Months in a Haunted House*, whatever was left of his personal fortune after the crash of 1929 and Marianne. Marianne had no money at all, Foyster and her 'sex urge'. While I do not believe that the bigamous marriage was planned in detail before a victim was available, I believe that the Foysters were on the lookout for a man whom they could ensnare, and then milk, from late 1934 onwards. Their peculiar sexual tastes would also have impelled them to do so; so the Foysters had two of the most powerful influences working upon them, sex and money. The victim was Henry Francis Fisher, whose involvement with the Foysters left him mad and penniless and on the wrong side of the law.

11

The Unlawfully Wedded Husband

Marianne could never have felt at home in the country; she needed towns for her hunting. Furthermore, to indulge in more escapades at Borley would have been to invite disaster. She and her husband could get away with d'Arles and the indoor sports of the haunting, but to repeat such activities in a small hamlet was to invite exposure and disaster. No doubt d'Arles's threat of blackmail gave both her and Lionel a nasty shock. Acting, therefore, according to her own peculiar logic, she transferred her other life from Wimbledon to Ipswich, the county town of Suffolk, which is only about thirty miles from Borley and, in Marianne's day, was easily accessible by train from Long Melford or Sudbury stations.

Visitors to Suffolk are usually surprised – disagreeably – by Ipswich. Suffolk boasts many beautiful small towns, such as Lavenham and the cathedral town of Bury St Edmunds, but Ipswich has more in common with an old-fashioned northern mill-town. It always was grim and unattractive, and modern housing developments have not helped its appearance. In Marianne's day it was a substantial port and was dominated by a power station, a gasworks and a brewery. Clearly Marianne did not go there to admire the scenery; Ipswich provided a substitute for London, where she could be lost in the crowds, assume a false identity and find ways of satisfying her urge to invent and live out her soap operas; and, of course, there were lots of men.

Marianne rented rooms, or a room, at 12 Gyppeswyck Road,

which is a cul-de-sac off Ancaster Road, and only a few minutes'
walk from Ipswich railway station. Gyppeswyck Road and the
adjoining streets consist of substantial, red-brick Victorian
houses, and the neighbourhood has suffered the usual
vicissitudes of such residential areas near the centres of English
cities. In the 1930s many of the houses were divided into flats
inhabited by poor working-class families. Now it is smart and
fashionable.

Marianne rented from Mrs Amy Saunders, with whom she
retained some connection until she left England in 1946. Mrs
Saunders rented out other properties nearby, including a
notorious house in Ranelagh Road that had degenerated into
such a slum by the late 1950s that although it was structurally
sound Ipswich Council demolished it and rehoused its teeming
inhabitants. Marianne rented a room here for a while in 1945-6,
as will be told in due course.

Trevor Hall visited Gyppeswyck Road in the mid-1950s, and a
lady in another house in the road remembered an attractive
dark-haired woman who had lived at No.12, and who called
herself by many names. This was without doubt Marianne, who,
when using her married name, called herself Miss Foyster or
Voyster. Hall's confidant also told him that the woman was often
visited by an elderly gentleman. Was this the magnificent
Santiago Monk, her 'spiritual godfather', come to her lodgings to
offer spiritual guidance?

Marianne was thus living in rented accommodation in
Ipswich, masquerading as a single woman, using a variety of
names, and as Foyster's wife, the chatelaine of Borley Rectory,
when she returned to that much-haunted hamlet. Foyster, we
must suppose, not only knew what she was up to but condoned
it. It has been suggested that the credulous, doting and simple
Foyster was deceived by various excuses, such as that
Marianne's absences were due to her engagement in charitable
work in London and elsewhere. This is absurd. If Foyster,
knowing what he already did about his wife, was prepared to
believe that her prolonged absences were attributable to such a
cause, he would have to have been quite mad, which he wasn't.

Marianne wasn't alone in Ipswich for long, for she soon met

Henry Francis Fisher. Fisher was an honest and honourable man. He wasn't another d'Arles. Fisher was his real name, and he really was a commercial traveller. He never claimed to be a spy. His problem was recurrent mental instability, attributed by his sister to a motor-cycle crash in his youth in which he had received head injuries. One thinks at once of Edwin Whitehouse, another man upon whom Marianne worked her charms, and who also had mental problems, in his case due to the Battle of Jutland. Fisher was completely taken in by Marianne (Miss Voyster) and later by that amateur father-in-law, the Rev. Lionel Algernon Foyster.

There was an exchange between Marianne and Swanson about her relationship with the luckless Fisher:

Swanson: Marianne, while you were at Borley Rectory one day, you met Henry Francis Fisher, whom you subsequently called Johnnie. You met him at the station?

Marianne: I believe it was either Colchester, or Marks Tey. We changed trains, I think it was Colchester, but it might have been Marks Tey, it was one of those stations. I was en route to London.

Swanson: Did you approach him or did he approach you, do you remember?

Marianne: I didn't approach him. We met – I think he asked me when the train went the other way and I told him I didn't know. Then we got talking and he asked me where I was going. I told him I was going to London.

Swanson: At this time you were married to Lionel Foyster?

Marianne: Yes, I was.

Swanson: You were not having any sexual relations with him because he was unable to?

Marianne: Yes.

Swanson: You made a date with Fisher to write to you at your flower shop or Borley?

Marianne: Yes, one of those places. I don't recall which one it was.

Swanson: Then he corresponded with you?

Marianne: Yes.

Swanson: And you met him at a hotel in London, is that right?

Marianne: Wait now – I – I did meet him at a hotel in London but I don't think that I – I don't think that I met – I do believe that it was at a hotel in London that I met him. I don't think that I met him anywhere before I met him at the hotel.

Swanson: Did you have relations with him at the hotel?

Marianne: Yes, I did.

Swanson: And you introduced Lionel Foyster as your father to him, is that correct?

Marianne: Yes, it is.

The questions and answers about the hotel are obscure. Marianne could of course have met Fisher during the later days of d'Arles and the flower shop, which is what the conversation appears to imply. On the other hand, even Marianne would have found it difficult to maintain a consistent and fraudulent persona to Fisher if they had been well acquainted during her London days. Fisher was based in Ipswich, and lodged at 38 London Road, a lodging house that catered for commercial travellers. It is therefore likely that in spite of the question-and-answer session with Swanson, Fisher and Marianne met when she was already based in Ipswich herself, living as the single Miss Foyster or Voyster in Gyppeswyck Road.

Fisher fell in love with Marianne, and they soon began an affair. She persuaded him to marry her by falsely claiming that she was pregnant. What exotic stories Fisher was told about her ancestry are sadly not known, but she did tell him one crucial lie, that Foyster was her father, and, amazing as this may seem, she even took him back to Borley and introduced him to Lionel as such. Clearly Foyster, this saintly religious man who is alleged to have suffered from a troubled conscience because he married a woman whom he had also baptized, cooperated. Again we see the different strands of Foyster's character that are woven through the whole Borley story: his love of play-acting, his anxiety about his material welfare and his tolerance of his wife's lovers.

Marianne later claimed that both she and Fisher were 'caught'; that is, she thought Fisher had money and Fisher thought she had money. The latter is not surprising, because Marianne probably told him all the fantastic tales about her aristocratic background that she told other people. It is a disservice to Fisher to suppose that he had any other motive than love for marrying Marianne. He, after all, clung pathetically to the relationship in later years, while she treated him quite shamelessly and cruelly, eventually leaving him penniless and demented. If anyone had ulterior motives connected with money it was almost certainly Marianne herself – and Foyster. Marianne had a lifelong habit of accusing others of exactly those things she had done herself, and her statement that Fisher was after money should be considered in this context. In summary, it appears that the Foysters' strange sexual and financial requirements were satisfied in the hapless person of Henry Francis Fisher.

*

Fisher came from a well-to-do family from the west of England. He was born at a country house named Michaelchurch Court at Michaelchurch, near Ross-on-Wye in Herefordshire, where his father had been a farmer. His date of birth was 22 December 1900, and he was thus almost two years younger than Marianne. After his final break with Marianne, and his complete emotional collapse in 1945, he retired into seclusion and never told his side of the story. He was cared for by his sister, and died at Worcester in the late 1960s.

Marianne was an accomplished and plausible liar, and acted without conscience. It is strange that her activities never took a more serious form than playing with people's emotions, and that she never came to the attention of the police for a serious crime. For this woman was capable not only of taking the unsuspecting Fisher to Borley and introducing him to Foyster as her father and Adelaide (her adopted daughter) as her sister, but also visited the Fisher family home in Michaelchurch. The mentality and resource of someone who is capable of imposing on so many people, with complete success, is truly extraordinary. It is strange also that she never appears to have found a creative outlet for her undoubted talents, leaving such matters as writing to her husband, who was no good at it at all, and relegating her acting abilities to cheap frauds and absurd indoor pursuits like the Borley ghosts. The only conclusion we can reach is that though her chosen lifestyle must have caused her great anxiety, with the ever present threat of exposure, she enjoyed it, just as she enjoyed violent sexual encounters with men such as d'Arles whom she didn't even like.

Taking Fisher to Borley was a great risk. It must have strained both Marianne's and Foyster's resources to the utmost. Incredible as it may seem, after the bigamous marriage Fisher and Marianne even lived at Borley with Foyster for a short while. Foyster was by now very ill indeed, and spent at least one long period in Long Melford nursing home. None the less the fact that Foyster and Marianne risked so much by having Fisher at Borley, even for a brief period, reinforces the impression that it was not only Marianne who derived sexual pleasure from her new relationship; Foyster, as remarked before, may have derived vicarious sexual pleasure from his wife's activities, and may even have been a voyeur.

*

The circumstances of the bigamous marriage are as follows: Henry Francis Fisher, described as a bachelor of 34 and a commercial traveller, married Marianne *Voyster*, described as a spinster of *30* and of no occupation, at St Pancras' Roman Catholic Church in Ipswich, on 23 February 1935. Fisher's father was described as a farmer, deceased; all the details relating to Fisher on the certificate are correct, but *every* detail about Marianne, with the exception of her Christian names, is false. Her father is Leon Alphonse Voyster, of independent means! She was, of course, born in 1899 and was therefore 36 at the time of the bigamous marriage.

The use of the name *Voyster*, and of the name Leon Alphonse for her father, are yet further indications of the way her mind worked when concocting frauds. Voyster is of course almost indistinguishable phonetically from Foyster. Her husband, Lionel Algernon, became her father, Leon Alphonse. The marriage took place before a priest in a Roman Catholic church, which suggests that Marianne's Roman Catholicism was not of the order of conventional religious faith. She was, in short, quite prepared to perjure herself not only in the eyes of the law, but also in the eyes of the church; and, a committed Catholic might say, in the very eyes of God.

Marianne falsely claimed she was pregnant to encourage Fisher to marry her. Instead of doing what most women would do under these circumstances and telling her husband that she had miscarried, Marianne adopted a new-born baby. (This arouses one's suspicions about the John (Evemond) Emery episode of 1932.) Given that Marianne gave the baby's birthday as 28 August 1935, her affair with Fisher must have started by December 1934. The amazing aspect of this, apart from Marianne's own behaviour, is that Fisher was taken in. I emphasise that Fisher seems to have acted from the best motives and was an innocent party to the bigamous marriage.

Trevor Hall got in touch with Fisher's sister in the 1950s, and it is from her that the available background information on the early stages of the relationship between her brother and Marianne comes. Her story confirms that Marianne did indeed call herself Miss Voyster, that outwardly she was a devout and enthusiastic Roman Catholic, that Foyster did impersonate his wife's father and that only later were Fisher's suspicions aroused about his 'wife' and 'father-in-law'. Of the many deceptions and impostures practised by this dangerous couple, the Fisher marriage is the worst, because it went on for so long, and involved not only Fisher but *two* adopted children whom Marianne presented to the world as her own. In addition to the little boy she adopted in 1935, she adopted a girl two years later. The boy she named John Henry Francis after Fisher (she disliked his Christian name and called him Johnnie), the girl Astrid Marianne Zaida. Both children were baptized in Roman

Catholic churches in Ipswich, John at St Pancras' on 22
September 1935 and Astrid at St Mary's on 22 March 1937.

A curious yet easily overlooked feature of this whole episode is
that Marianne bothered to indulge in these elaborate and
dangerous pantomimes instead of abandoning Foyster who, she
agreed, was no use to her sexually. With her resources, there
was surely no obstacle to continuing her career of confidence
tricks *and* being rid of the old Rector. Yet she appears to have
clung to him, carefully involved him with everything and later
continued to care for him when he was crippled and bedridden.
There was a strong bond between them which lasted almost to
the end; it appears to be connected with their father-daughter
relationship, which they actually lived out together in an
atmosphere charged with rapacious sexuality. Again, one cannot
help but wonder about the relationship between little Marianne
and the curate back in Cheshire before the First World War.

The Fishers made their first married home at Borley, until, in
July 1935, Marianne and Henry Francis moved back to Ipswich,
to 4 Ancaster Road, a large house next to the railway station: it
is now a guest house, and interested readers may like to spend a
night or two there and imagine the workings of this
extraordinary household. Henry Francis went to stay with his
family in Michaelchurch during August, and there he received a
telegram from Marianne, who had retired to Borley for her
imaginary confinement, which informed him: 'It's a boy!'

Marianne obtained children from adoption societies with
frightening ease; one wonders how many other babies were
obtained by mad, unstable or otherwise unsuitable people
during the 1930s. Marianne herself was never very clear about
how she got hold of them, though she was questioned about this
by Swanson. They had several exchanges on this matter,
Marianne claiming first that she had used the London Adoption
Society and then the adoption service run by the Church of
England. I have met John Fisher, who eventually traced his real
mother. She told him that she was told that her baby was to be
adopted by a charming Rector's wife and would have a new life
in Canada. Clearly (and not surprisingly) Marianne was
Munchausening at the adoption clinic.

In October 1935 Foyster retired from Borley on grounds of ill-health – he had suffered that famous collapse in the pulpit while he was 'hollering about sin' – and went to join the household at Ancaster Road as his wife's father, a role he was now to play for the rest of his life. The family, consisting of three adults, Adelaide (who must have been utterly confused by this time, for she had lived through not only the Borley 'haunting', but also her own transformation into her adopted mother's sister) and the baby John, lived here until the autumn of 1936. In September of that year they moved into a new bungalow at 102 Woodbridge Road East, which was, at this time, situated in a surburb on the northern edge of the town, adjacent to Rushmere Common and golf-course. The area has suffered since from road-widening schemes and heavy traffic, but in Marianne's day it must have been a pleasant place to live. According to Fisher's sister, the house was paid for by the Fisher family; thus the Foysters' financial and sexual speculations had paid off, handsomely.

The house still stands, and still has the windows in the roof which give light to two small rooms; it was in one of these that Foyster took up his abode and continued to work on his masterpiece, *Fifteen Months in a Haunted House*. Fisher's sister said that her mother stayed in the bungalow for at least one holiday of several weeks, and not once during this time did she see the mysterious 'Old Mr Voyster' up in his eerie. She tried to gain access to the room when Marianne was out, but it was locked. It has been suggested that Foyster was under house-arrest during this period. This cannot be true. He was in touch with the outside world, corresponding with, among others, Sydney Glanville, and he could easily have asked his Bull or Foyster relatives for assistance had he so desired. His room remained locked up because he was as anxious as Marianne not to be found out; his material welfare depended on the continuing deception of the Fishers.

An interesting vignette of the family life at Woodbridge Road East was provided by a former neighbour who, in the 1950s, remembered Mr and Mrs Fisher who sometimes took out Mrs Fisher's elderly and crippled father for rides in the car. Henry

Francis Fisher must have been a great relief after the Rabelaisian François d'Arles. We recall that Foyster himself was moved to remark to Mrs Fenton of Wimbledon that he was so glad that she had got rid of him and found a 'nice chap' like Fisher.

While the Fishers were at Woodbridge Road East, Harry Price's investigators and teams of observers were haunting Borley in the hope of seeing a ghost. We have already met Mr Sydney H. Glanville and his children, Roger and Helen. When Glanville began his own investigation into the background of the Borley haunting he not unnaturally wanted to talk to the Foysters about their experiences. We recall that he sought out the Smiths and the Misses Bull. He happened to know Foyster's brother Arthur Henry, who lived in Pinner, and wrote to him to enquire whether Lionel Algernon would be prepared to help with the investigation. On 28 August 1937 Arthur Foyster replied:

Dear Mr Glanville, Your letter very much surprised me, as I had understood from my brother that during the last years of his stay at B——— the phenomena had entirely ceased. Prof. Cook of Cambridge whom I met at Aldeburgh, told me that he had been to B——— and investigated the matter, while the phenomena were supposed to be active, and found there was nothing in it.

I am afraid that I know nothing about it at first hand but I am writing to my brother to ask him whether he would care to send you any details. He is now crippled with rheumatism and I would fancy that writing is rather an effort, so he may not want to do so.

Prof. Cook was apparently rather keen on these sort of things and only came to the conclusions he did after a very thorough investigation of the full particulars he got and with great disappointment.

With kind regards,
Yours sincerely,
(signed) A.H. Foyster

P.S. I never mentioned to my brother that I met Prof. Cook

as I understand that Cook's conclusions very much annoyed
him.

As an aside, readers may care to know that Cook's opinions
are never mentioned in the orthodox Borley literature. On 31
August, Foyster himself wrote to Glanville from 102 Woodbridge
Road East, Ipswich. His letter briefly summarised the events
already recorded in his *Diary of Experiences*:

> Dear Sir, I heard from my brother yesterday that you had
> written to him about B——— Rectory asking for any
> information that might help you in your investigations. I
> am therefore writing to you to tell you something about our
> experiences while I was rector of B———.
> I lived in the Rectory from 1930 – 1935. That time, as far
> as phenomena are concerned, was divided into two periods.
> *First*. October 1930, when we came into residence, to Jan.
> 1932 when we finally got the house settled by a spiritualist
> circle aided by a medium they had procured – who I think
> did most of it. During this period we had, what were to me,
> almost unbelievable experiences.

Foyster then went on to his summary of 'phenomena',
modestly omitting to mention that he was still enjoying almost
unbelievable experiences at 102 Woodbridge Road East while he
impersonated his wife's father and hid in his room from Fisher's
inquisitive mother.

> For the first few months – up to February 1931 – there were
> odd happenings, but not much of great consequence. But in
> February 1931 a campaign of frightfulness started and kept
> on intermittently until Jan. 1932.

The reader will recall that March 1931 was the date of
d'Arles's advent at the unquiet Rectory.

> It would take too long to give any details, but it included
> stones, bottles, and all sorts of other articles thrown round

(this often happened in broad daylight or good artificial light, and with doors and windows shut); bells rung, rooms turned upside down, doors locked and keys taken away, things moved and sometimes taken away for good, while other articles we had never seen before appeared, people struck – and more or less seriously injured; unaccountable noises and smells (some of the latter when the powers of good were in the ascendant were very delicious); an ill person turned out of bed (three times in one day); also occasional apparitions.

I was never seriously hurt, but my wife was; neither (not being psychic) did I ever see anything, though present with people who could. I must not omit the writings; 'Get light mass prayers here' was written upon the walls in different places and probably is still visible.

Second. The spiritualist circle and the medium spent the best part of a night in the house in January 1932 and subsequently the phenomena ceased entirely, except for one or two little demonstrations hardly worth noticing. It was absolutely a different house. Shortly before we left, however, there were some signs of things starting up again, but nothing in any way comparable to what we had experienced. So I am afraid the best time for investigating the phenomena is passed.

However a member of the circle who takes a great interest in the house, told me last year that he considered the place was by no means clear of spirits yet; also that there was an 'elemental' in the cellar.

If there is any further information I can give, please let me know. Trusting what I have told you will be of some use,

Yours faithfully,
(signed) L.A. Foyster

The correspondence with Glanville continued, Glanville sending Foyster a list of questions about the haunting and Foyster replying on 2 September:

Dear Mr Glanville, I am glad the information I sent you about B——— was of some use. I am very interested to hear that you have already been there. The message 'light etc,' I think is also in the bathroom passage. 'Marianne' is my wife's name.

This last sentence removes any doubts about Foyster's mental decay having advanced to such a stage that he truly did not know who Marianne really was – which might have been the case were he suffering from Alzheimer's disease. His letter continues with a detailed description of the 'phenomena' in which the ghost of Harry Bull, his wife's psychic powers and the legend of the nun all appear. Finally, in a letter dated 12 September, Foyster got round to the subject of his novel. This clearly meant a great deal to him, and perhaps he still entertained serious hopes that he would not only succeed in finding a publisher but also make some money out of it. Foyster asked Glanville to read the manuscript (180 type-written pages) and give his opinion.

Glanville duly read Foyster's novel, and wrote to him on 8 October, describing it as 'the most astonishing document I have ever read', but being tactfully evasive about its chances of publication. He also wrote: 'I am sorry that it does not seem possible for us to talk the matter over.' Foyster did not wish to receive visitors at Woodbridge Road East.

Price and Foyster later corresponded, when Price, who was embarking on his own, ultimately highly successful, literary venture was soliciting Foyster for his first-hand accounts of his life at Borley. Foyster's initial frosty reply of 7 January 1938 has already been quoted on p. 46. Later in the same letter, in reply to Price's inquiries about his health, Foyster mentions that he cannot walk. His replies to Price's letters became warmer, and eventually he sent him the material he wanted, his *Summary of Experiences*, which has been quoted in full on pp. 36-43 above. Price already had access to Foyster's *Diary of Occurrences*, which covered the period from the Foysters' arrival at Borley to July 1931.

Foyster clung to the hope that his own book might be published even after Price's first Borley work, *The Most Haunted House in England*, had appeared in 1940. Indeed his reason for dealing with the man who had so offended him during their one and only meeting was that Foyster, like Mrs Smith before him, hoped that Price might put him in touch with a publisher, something which Price had absolutely no intention of doing. In a letter to Price dated 5 December 1940 Foyster wrote:

Thank you very much for returning my MS and for promising to let me know if you hear of any chance of someone wanting to take it.

Like all aspiring authors, Foyster clung to every hope, however slender; of course Price made use of what he had read for his second Borley book, *The End of Borley Rectory*. In his letters to Price Foyster frequently refers to his poor health. The picture that emerges is of a broken-down man, who writes of 'elementals' in cellars, who is bedridden and who can only write with difficulty because his hands are badly crippled and he has to prop up the paper on his knee in bed.

How much did Foyster's relations, the Bulls and his brothers, Bernard and Arthur, know about what was going on? Clearly Arthur Foyster was dropping tactful hints to Glanville that the haunting wasn't worth further investigation. But how much did they know about Foyster's domestic arrangements? John Fisher has told me that Marianne kept his relations away from him during his last days. At Borley, however, the Misses Bull, those cantankerous spinsters, were frequent visitors.

The only hint about what they may have known or suspected is given in *The Locked Book*. Glanville records:

Regarding the Rev. L.A. Foyster and Mrs Marianne Foyster: They expressed the definite opinion that Mrs Marianne Foyster is a 'medium' and that psychic phenomena occurs [*sic*] in her presence, wherever she happens to be.

She adopted two children, one of them, Adelaide has now (1938) entered the Roman Catholic church. At this date, June 1938, she has apparently adopted two more children. All these children were adopted without payment.

Her husband has always been, and still is, infatuated with her. He seems to count every moment that she is absent from him.

They remember François d'Arles and agree that he was an 'extraordinary' man.

Miss Ethel Bull describes Mrs Marianne Foyster as 'mad as a hatter' and her sister says that she was 'a little beast'.

The Misses Bull knew that Marianne had acquired a family since she left Borley, but had been told, correctly, that the children had been adopted. Marianne could hardly have claimed that they were Lionel's, because it would have been evident, even to the Misses Bull, that he was incapable of fathering them. Finally, although we can understand why one of her cousins-by-marriage said that Marianne was as mad as a hatter, we long to know what she'd done to the other one who described her as a little beast. There is a hint here that the Misses Bull might have had some idea of what was going on behind the scenes at Borley. Indeed it would have been strange if these suspicious and nasty old ladies hadn't ferreted something out. Perhaps they appreciated the irony of their accusations against their sister-in-law, Ivy Bull. For not only had their cousin Lionel been entangled in a bigamous marriage, he was to be hastened on his way by his wife in much the same manner as Harry was said to have been despatched by the wicked Ivy.

12

A Pastoral Intermezzo

The Fishers and their dependants, the three children and that agreeable old gentleman Mr Foyster, stayed at the house in Ipswich until June 1938, when they moved to a remote village north of Woodbridge. Given that the bungalow had been paid for by Fisher, or Fisher's family, this move after only nineteen months is odd; for they rented Hill Farm House, at Chillesford, for £40 a year, instead of buying another house.

Marianne later claimed that the move was because Lionel did not like the bungalow in Ipswich; the traffic irritated him, his wheelchair was difficult to manoeuvre in the relatively small house, the neighbours could see him when he was in the garden, and anyway he wanted to live in the country. Though these reasons are plausible, and might have contributed to the decision to leave surburban Ipswich, the choice of Chillesford is suggestive. Even today, when the population of Suffolk has greatly increased and the county has undergone several post-war booms, Chillesford can still be described as remote and isolated. It lies on the margins of Tunstall Forest, not far from Orford, and owes its present somewhat cosmopolitan character to the nearby American airbase of Bentwaters. This, of course, did not exist when Marianne and her family moved there.

Foyster had been contacted by ghost hunters. As we have seen, Sydney Glanville had even proposed meeting him at his home. Furthermore Foyster was a well-known figure in Ipswich; the household may therefore have had other reasons than those given by Marianne for taking itself off to a tiny village.

Significantly they moved twice again after their move to Chillesford, both times to other remote and lonely houses.

Hill Farm still stands today; it is a large, red-brick farmhouse, with high roofs, standing well back from the road, and has a striking similarity to Borley Rectory as the latter appears in old photographs (see Plate 1). In the 1950s, people at Chillesford still remembered Mr and Mrs Fisher and said that Mr Fisher was away a lot, that Mrs Fisher's old father Mr Foyster was bedridden and rarely seen and that the children were badly neglected. The neglect of the children is curious, because Marianne has always maintained that she adopted them because she loved children and had despaired of having any of her own. The stories of her neglect and cruelty come not only from the former neighbours but from John Fisher himself. Marianne frequently beat them, and devised punishments such as sticking their heads into buckets of cold water for what seem to have been dangerously long period of time. As will be told later, Marianne abandoned them when she fled to America in 1946.

That exposure was an ever-present threat is shown by Marianne's choice of another Roman Catholic church in Ipswich, St Mary's, for the baptism of Astrid Marianne Zaida, in 1937. The registers of this church also show that Henry Francis Fisher was conditionally baptized there the following year. In such circumstances most people would have used the city church where they had been married. It is important to understand that Marianne presented the children to the priests as her own and with false dates of birth. Although this does not invalidate their baptisms, it is highly suggestive of Marianne's attitude to her faith. She lied to priests in the most shameless fashion and yet presented an exterior of devout and militant catholicism. Not only did she convert the luckless Fisher, but the reader will remember that she also tried to convert her nurse-companion at Borley, Miss Dytor.

They remained at Chillesford until 22 May 1940, when they moved again, this time to a large detached house, The Whin, in the village of Snape a few miles from Aldeburgh. In those days before the annual music festival, Snape was as remote as

Chillesford; again there is the suspicion that the Foysters were trying to hide.

Their stay at Snape was a peculiar interlude, even by their standards, for here Fisher was not in evidence; Marianne and Lionel lived as Mr and Mrs Foyster, man and wife. During the latter days at Chillesford, Fisher had given up his job as a commercial traveller (he is described by his sister as having been employed by a Yorkshire ironmongery firm, and by 'Harris's Cake' by Marianne), and is said to have worked in a 'war factory' at Saxmundham, a town about ten miles away. According to his sister, his absence during the Snape period was due to his stay in hospital suffering from duodenal trouble – again in Saxmundham. His illness, even if prolonged, would not, however, account for Marianne's sudden reversion to the title Mrs Foyster. The implication is that there had been a breach with Fisher. He may have suffered one of his breakdowns because of this, or because he had discovered the true horror of his situation.

His sister has said that their mother tried to see Mr Foyster (or Voyster) at the Ipswich bungalow but his door was always locked. The Fisher family must have realised that there was something strange about Marianne and her 'father'. The sister also said that Foyster would sometimes refer to Marianne as his wife and then quickly correct himself. Marianne explained this oddity by stating that her father sometimes wandered in his head and said the strangest things. Fisher's sister said that Fisher had doubts about the paternity of Astrid, which suggests that Marianne was unfaithful to him, and that he knew it. The most likely explanation of Marianne's reversion to her true married name at Snape is, therefore, that there had been trouble with Fisher, whose doubts could no longer be contained, and that he had suffered a mental breakdown. Perhaps Marianne was preparing herself for the worst – exposure. The lady from whom the Foysters rented The Whin stated that it had always seemed odd to her that Mrs Foyster appeared to have no friends, and that no one called at the house. Price's first Borley book appeared in 1940, and this of course made much of the experiences of Foyster and his psychic wife. In spite of the war it was a bestseller and attracted much attention. Fisher may have read it and realised the truth about his wife and father-in-law. Price's book was published in August, several months after the move to Snape; thus the book itself could not have been the reason for Fisher's absence. On the other hand, Marianne later (during the interviews with Swanson) expressed great animosity towards Price. The most likely explanation of her attitude towards the great investigator is that the publication of his first book caused her a great deal of domestic trouble.

In spite of his suspicions, Fisher clung to the relationship, for in June 1941 Marianne moved her family again, this time to the most remote and inhospitable of all their houses, Dairy Cottage in Rendelsham; here she was again Mrs Fisher, and in the 1950s neighbours remembered her husband Mr Fisher, who was away from Rendelsham a great deal. Mrs Fisher's old, bedridden father was never seen. Several children were there, including an evacuee named Downing.

A visit to Dairy Cottage will convince the reader that Marianne was trying to hide herself, and that concealment, as much as her natural restlessness, was her reason for moving there. Dairy Cottage, a two-storey, red-brick building about half a mile up a narrow lane off the Rendelsham-to-Campsea-Ashe road, has hardly changed since 1945; the single building is divided internally into two, and was originally used to house workers from the Rendelsham Hall estate. Bentwaters airbase is not far away, but in Marianne's day there was nothing but Tunstall Forest and a few other cottages, none of them less than half a mile from her new home.

Since Marianne never showed any consideration for Fisher, it is not unreasonable to suppose that her main preoccupation, when his suspicions developed into something more substantial, was fear of exposure. She had committed a serious crime. The neighbours at Rendelsham to whom Trevor Hall spoke in the 1950s told him that the Fishers had an elder daughter, who was away at boarding school and whom they had never seen. This was Adelaide, and Marianne must have been anxious to remove her from Fisher's immediate presence once his suspicions were aroused. Adelaide had been with the Foysters since their

Canadian days, had lived through the Borley 'phenomena' with them and was in a position, if questioned by an adult, to give the game away.

That Marianne was looking for an escape route is shown by her escapade with Dr Davies of the Grosvenor Hotel, Victoria, with whom she became involved in the autumn of 1941. His story is interesting because, as far as I know, he is the only male victim to have spoken at length about his relationship with her. His account shows how cruel and ruthless Marianne could be in her dealings with men; she displayed the moral sensibilities of a large predator on the African Savannah.

Dr Davies, according to his own account, had worked in a general medical practice in the Midlands. His wife, Mabel, to whom he was devoted, died of cancer, leaving him grief-stricken. He appears to have suffered a complete emotional collapse, which, if the reader remembers the medical history of Edwin Whitehouse and Henry Francis Fisher, made him an ideal victim for Marianne. She seems never to have sought out the company of balanced, healthy males. Although she was obliged to prey on the weak and unstable, by virtue of her own fantasy life and her inability to tell the truth, it is curious that she *never* felt the need, or was not impelled by the need, to find a satisfying relationship that was based on mutual trust and which had the slightest prospect of enduring. The implication of this is that such needs as she did have in this sense were satisfied by Foyster, who, I believe, was fully in her confidence at every stage of their relationship. Marianne never made lasting friendships with either men or women because she told lies which, sooner or later, obliged her to retreat lest she be found out. This fear of exposure was always paramount. She never took even a female friend into her confidence. One would imagine that when her life had become so complicated by her deceptions and impostures that it became unsustainable, she would have needed the advice and affection of at least one true friend, whether male or female; yet her response to the difficulties that her lies and games caused her was to tell still more lies in an attempt to escape from the consequences.

The extent of Davies's grief and the completeness of his

emotional collapse are indicated by his abandonment of his practice in the Midlands and move to the Grosvenor Hotel, Victoria, where, like many bereaved persons, he interested himself in spiritualism with the object of making contact with his dead wife. He did not work, but lived on capital. He read up on spiritualism, and of course came across the works of Harry Price. The two met. Then disaster befell poor Davies, for he read *The Most Haunted House in England* and came to the conclusion that Marianne Foyster was clearly the most powerful medium who had ever lived. The reader will remember that as well as allegedly witnessing the most spectacular 'phenomena', Marianne was credited with being 'psychic'. Davies asked Price for Marianne's address, and wrote to her. A meeting followed, in London. Davies had fallen into the trap.

When they first met, Davies was forty-five and Marianne forty-two. He described her as an 'exceedingly attractive woman, looking not a day older than the mid-thirties. She was of medium height and build, with an excellent figure and the most graceful movements. She was dark-haired with a round face and regular features.'

Davies said that Marianne's eyes were her most striking feature; they were dark, shining and luminous. Her lips were thick and sensuous. She was witty and vivacious and could converse on a wide variety of subjects, and spoke French fluently. She gave the general impression of being well-educated. Davies caught some warning signs at least, for he said that when she was looking at him when she thought he wasn't observing her, there was 'something satanic' about her regard. Nevertheless he became infatuated with her. The omniscient Swanson questioned Marianne about her relationship with Davies:

Swanson: Marianne, do you recall Dr Davies?
Marianne: Yes.
Swanson: Did you ever have sexual relations with him?
Marianne: No, I did not. The matter never came up in any way. On my first interview with him, he told me that I was a dead ringer for his wife, he said that her name was

Tweatie and that she'd died of cancer. I thought at the
time he was mentally retarded, due to the recent loss of a
beloved person. The second time I saw him was at the
Grosvenor Hotel. I had lunch with him. At this time he
suggested that we go to a medium in Hampstead that he
knew of, but I refused. That sort of thing always makes
me feel ill.

Marianne is lying. If 'that sort of thing' always made her feel
ill, what was she doing meeting Davies in the first place? And
what of her claims during the Borley period? She met Davies on
many occasions in London. He paid her train fare from Wickham
Market (the nearest railway station to Rendelsham), and they
paid a visit to the offices of the Society for Psychical Research,
then in Tavistock Square (it was because an official of the
Society remembered them that Davies was traced by Hall).
When they visited the Society, Marianne was 'very flashily
dressed' and she and Davies appeared to be on 'very friendly
terms'.

Davies became infatuated with her, and she targeted him as
she had targeted Fisher and other victims. Given Davies's
mental condition, this was cruel and ruthless. Davies insisted
that nothing improper occurred between them, but given that he
lived for years in the fear that she would blackmail him this
seems unlikely. Marianne would not have been able (especially
in wartime) to make day trips from Wickham Market to London
that included dinner and shows. Davies admitted that she did,
on occasion, stay overnight at his hotel, but that his devotion to
his dead wife's memory gave him the strength to resist the
obvious temptation.

Marianne's statement that spiritualism made her feel ill is
also hard to understand given Davies's account of how she fell
into a trance in the hotel lounge and attempted automatic writing. Davies's scruples about being faithful to his dead wife appear
to have been overcome by an ingenious stratagem that both
parties no doubt found satisfactory. Marianne began by embracing him when she was in a trance, when, of course, it could be
argued that it was not Marianne's arms which were around

him but those of dear departed Tweatie. Alas for the flesh; for embraces followed when Marianne was *not* in a trance and when Tweatie was very definitely on the 'other side'. That Marianne could coldly exploit this man is both frightening and revealing.

Marianne told Davies the truth about her circumstances, which is surprising. She said that her husband, Lionel Foyster, to whom she referred by the pet-name of 'Lion', was not expected to live long, and she showed a great interest in Dr Davies's material circumstances. While omitting to mention the existence of Fisher, she did vouchsafe the interesting intelligence that 'Lion' had no growl left in him.

Marianne was of course obliged to present herself to Davies as Mrs Foyster, because he had read Price's books. Her use of him, however, indicates that she realised that her adventures with both Fisher and Foyster were coming to an end. She was anticipating Foyster's death. That her interest in Davies was material as well as sexual is indicated by her questions about his financial situation.

The relationship with Davies lasted six months, until he told her that his capital was running low, upon which Marianne abruptly became less enthusiastic. She wrote to him in March 1942, saying that their relationship was over; he returned the many love-letters she had written and requested that she do the same. She never returned them, and thus the unfortunate doctor lived for many years dreading that he was going to be blackmailed.

Marianne's final touch is astounding. Davies had given her many of his dead wife's clothes, and she returned these to him twisted into strange doll-like shapes, with mysterious pieces of cardboard upon which what Davies described as 'cabbalistic symbols' were inscribed. Not unnaturally he gained the impression that Marianne was trying to place a curse on him. This incident, more than any other, shows Marianne's cruel and vindictive nature. Again, one wonders that she never ended up in court, accused of a serious crime.

Edwin Whitehouse, Henry Francis Fisher and Dr Davies were all disturbed men. The pattern of their relationships with Marianne is the same. Infatuation is followed by exploitation through the most ridiculous impostures: the writing on the walls, the bigamous marriage and the charade of the adopted boy, the trances and embraces in the lounge of the Grosvenor Hotel. Finally there is a crisis that results in more or less total breakdown. Foyster never suffered a similar breakdown, so far as one can tell. The implication is that his relationship with Marianne was of a different order. The other men fell apart when they were forced to recognise Marianne's true nature. That Foyster suffered no such climax supports the theory that he and Marianne were always in each other's confidence and acted in concert. Foyster could not be disillusioned because he knew what she was like and rejoiced in his association with her.

Marianne's attitude to the men she exploited is interesting; she acted as if she were totally devoid of any sympathy with them, almost as if she were deliberately encompassing their downfall. Do we see in this something of Foyster himself? If he was impotent, as seems likely, and preoccupied with sin and sex, as Marianne herself has claimed, he might have exulted at this exploitation and abuse of sinful, sexually potent men who, for all their ability to pleasure his sexually rapacious wife, acted blindly and stupidly walked into the traps that had been set for them.

But though Marianne had protected Foyster in the past, she told Dr Davies that he wouldn't live long. The double act was over. Now Foyster, twisted with arthritis and bedridden, was a liability. In view of what was to happen at Dairy Cottage in 1945, Marianne's words have an ominous ring.

13

Eisenhower's Sweetheart

From early 1942 onwards Marianne's position became increasingly precarious. Fisher was declining towards his final breakdown, which, she must have realised, would precipitate a family scandal and could well lead to her exposure. The incontinent, bedridden Foyster was in decline but clinging to life and showing no signs of doing the decent thing and taking himself off to the 'other side' to enjoy the company of Tweatie, Harry Bull and the murdered nun of Borley. She had told so many lies to so many people that continued social contact with anyone whom she knew well and who might be relied upon to help her was difficult if not impossible; and her project with Dr Davies had failed.

But help was at hand. The Yanks were coming! The cavalry was riding to the rescue in the shape of the American Eighth Air Force which, after the United States entered the war in December 1941, began a massive programme of building airfields ('airdromes') in Norfolk and Suffolk, from which their Flying Fortresses and Liberators could mount their great assault on the German war machine. The new airfields were known as 'Class A Bomber Fields' and, by the standards of the time, were huge. So many were built that often their perimeters were only one or two miles apart; the runways consisted of a vast elliptical perimeter track, a main take-off runway more than a mile long, and two auxiliary runways. They had mess halls, barrack huts, movie theatres, their own electricity and sewage plants, and complements of about two thousand lonely

American servicemen, all of them well-supplied with fruit, choc-
olates, nylon stockings, cigarettes, drink and, of course, money.
By British standards, US servicemen were fabulously wealthy.
The surprising aspect of Marianne's involvement with them is
not that she found one of her own, but that it took her so long. He
was Private Robert Vincent O'Neil, Serial Number 47097995,
who was born in Caledonia, Minnesota, on 22 February 1920 and
enlisted at Fort Snelling on 13 January 1941. His foreign service
dates are recorded as 1 September 1943 to 25 December 1945.

O'Neil was based at the field of the 390th Heavy Bombardment
Group at Parham (Framlingham), which was a Flying Fortress
unit of great distinction. O'Neil was not a crewman, but a member
of the ground complement. A barracks for American servicemen
was set up in Rendlesham Park, and although O'Neil was billeted
at Parham it seems that he had occasion to go to Rendlesham and
thus pass by Dairy Cottage.

Marianne claimed that she met him when Foyster was taken ill
('had made a collapse'). Because their regular British civilian
doctor, K.J.T. Keer MRCS of Wickham Market (of whom more
anon) was not available, she had been obliged to ask for assistance from the nearby camp. Marianne later made a feeble
attempt to weave a 'Dr O'Neil' into a story, but O'Neil was not a
doctor, he was a private soldier. Some GIs, including O'Neil,
visited Dairy Cottage to see what they could do to help, and from
this beginning the relationship developed.

Inevitably the efficient and ruthless Swanson questioned
Marianne about her great GI romance:

Swanson: How did you meet him?
Marianne: I was introduced to him by someone else. Lionel
    had made a collapse and I had gone to get the Army
    doctor who came and administered temporary measures
    until I could get Dr Keer, our regular physician. I think
    that this was how I met him, then two soldiers came to
    ask me how Lionel was – and that is how I met Robert.
Swanson: Did he stay in the cottage overnight?
Marianne: Yes, he stayed there two or three times and we
    did have sexual relations.

Swanson: At this time Fisher was away and you had a sexual urge again?

Marianne: Yes, I did.

Swanson: How long were you at Dairy Cottage before Lionel died?

Marianne: Two or three years.

Swanson: Did O'Neil ever meet Fisher?

Marianne: No.

Swanson: Did he know that you were married to Fisher?

Marianne: Yes, because people had told him. Then, too, I was called Mrs Fisher.

Swanson: Marianne, you have always had a very peculiar and very strong sex desire, is that true?

Marianne: Yes, it comes upon me – and it's almost overwhelming, but it is sort of sporadic, if you know what I mean.

Swanson: At those times you have to have a man, is that true?

Marianne: I don't suppose that I should say I have to because you don't have to do anything, but I am desperate during this period.

Swanson: Was it a matter of sex desperation when you first met O'Neil?

Marianne: The first time that I had relations with Bob I was under the influence of too much drink.

Swanson: Did you see an opportunity in O'Neil to plan to come back to America?

Marianne: Yes, Lionel always said that I should go back to America, and I promised him that I would. Lionel said that O'Neil and I seemed to get along well together and one day he said, 'When I am dead, why don't you marry O'Neil and go to America?'

Swanson: What did Lionel think of the marriage between Fisher and you?

Marianne: He said that I could get that annulled.

John Fisher, who was sent away to a Catholic boarding school in Ipswich but who returned to Dairy Cottage at weekends, told me that O'Neil was a frequent visitor. The GI was liberal with sweets for the children and drink for Marianne; he installed a barrel of beer in the larder. He also had a car (this must have been from the motor pool at Parham, since GIs were not allowed private vehicles). O'Neil was kind and indulgent with the children.

John Fisher has supplied the following accounts of his childhood:

I first knew Marianne Fisher as my mother when we lived at Chillesford, Suffolk. We referred to the Reverend Foyster as 'Fafa' and Mrs Fisher was never 'mother' or 'mummy' to us, but we called her 'Morny'. From Chillesford we moved to a large house in Snape, Suffolk and from there to Dairy Cottage, Rendlesham, Suffolk, where we spent most of the war years. During my childhood I remember various other children being part of the household, but can only recall the names and faces of about four. One girl I vaguely remember was Adelaide Foyster, several years older than myself.

'Fafa' was an invalid and I spent quite a lot of time in his room at Rendlesham reading to him and writing his letters. I enjoyed his company and though he was sick in body, in my young opinion he had a very lively mind. Also his room was a refuge from the beatings and bad temper of Mrs Fisher.

Mrs Fisher had some men callers – one was an Irishman, another was the American Air Force man O'Neil and there was a Johnny Fisher. I remember little about him except that 'Morny' threatened me, 'If you don't behave yourself, I'll send you to Johnny Fisher.'

At Rendelsham I remember my younger sister, Astrid Fisher, though she spent most of the time in a convent in Braintree, Essex and the few times she was home she always seemed to be ill in bed. Nevertheless we kept in touch for a few years by writing to each other. There were also two evacuees with us at Rendelsham, David and Stewart Downing and their father Sergeant Downing from Bromley Kent would visit them and seemed much taken with Mrs Fisher. In fact I believe that he wanted to marry her.

In another account John Fisher wrote:

> Henry Fisher visited Dairy Cottage while I was there, and was known to me as 'Johnny Fisher'. Strangely enough I did not think of him as a relative, but just as a visitor, even though my own name was 'John Fisher'. It is quite likely that Henry Fisher stayed at Dairy Cottage during the times I was at boarding school. As far back as I can remember Marianne called herself Mrs Fisher and I was once asked whether the elderly person who lived with us was my grandfather, but as I did not know myself, I decided that being a minister, he must be my god-father. Rev. Foyster was certainly bedridden and stayed in one room all the time at Rendelsham. His arms and legs were drawn up with arthritis. I used to like to spend some time with Rev. Foyster and can remember writing letters for him and feeding him with an invalid cup.

Becoming one of 'Eisenhower's Sweethearts' (as the British GI brides were called) offered Marianne about the only way out of the *reductio ad absurdum* that her life had become. She was in a corner. She had contracted a bigamous marriage and was on the threshold of exposure by the wronged man's family. The children she had adopted and falsely claimed to be her own were now an encumbrance and had to be kept in boarding schools. And Foyster was still alive, bedridden and helpless. Marianne's escape from this situation was her master-stroke.

Her first job was to dispose of Foyster. John Fisher has told of how Foyster was shamefully neglected during his last days, and therefore 'disposing' of him might have meant no more than locking him up and waiting for him to die of neglect. On the other hand, given that Marianne was desperate, she might have pushed a pillow over his face. Foyster's relatives had become very concerned about him towards the end, but were unable to gain access to him. In John Fisher's words, they were 'not at all

happy about the circumstances of his death'. Strange to say,
Foyster's spirit performed a regular turn at amateur seances in
the late 1940s, bemoaning his murder while in mortal life. There
were even rumours that Foyster himself was haunting Borley.
Fisher's sister claimed that Foyster was poisoned.

Foyster died on 18 April 1945, of 'exhaustion, bedsores, and
rheumatoid arthritis'. The death certificate was signed by K.J.T.
Keer, MRCS. The place of death was Dairy Cottage,
Rendlesham, and Marianne Foyster was present at the death.

Although at first sight the certificate appears to be in order,
the stated causes of death are odd. No one dies from bed sores;
bed sores can cause septicaemia, but then the cause of death is
septicaemia not bed sores. 'Exhaustion' is stranger still. Most
invalids who die are exhausted, but exhaustion cannot, without
qualification, be given as a cause of death. I have discussed
Foyster's death certificate with several doctors; all of them
considered the causes to be insufficient. Keer's signature is not
as impressive as it might be when Marianne's hold over a local
solicitor is known. This solicitor was employed to track
Marianne down by a woman upon whom one of the children was
later dumped. He had no luck. Yet he was the very solicitor who
helped Marianne prove Foyster's will at the probate office in
1946, before she left the country. That the solicitor was corrupt
(even by the usual standards of his profession) is beyond doubt;
but what is interesting is the nature of the hold that Marianne
had over him. When we consider her involvement with Dr
Davies of the Grosvenor Hotel, the possibility suggests itself
that she had entangled him in an affair and blackmailed him.
She may well have done the same with the doctor, who was
obliged to keep quiet about any doubts he might have had about
the circumstances of Foyster's death and sign a certificate. The
insufficient causes may have been his equivalent of a child's
crossing its fingers when making a promise it does not intend to
keep.

I am convinced that Marianne did hasten Foyster's end. In his
last minutes he may have regretted giving Marianne that advice
about marrying the American soldier and going back to
America. The pressures on Marianne were by this time

intolerable, and she knew that there was no escape as long as she was burdened with her husband. The end of the European war was in sight, and O'Neil would soon be posted overseas or returned to the United States.

Trevor Hall, on the basis of circumstantial evidence, and Swanson (a former US law enforcement official), on the basis of his interviews with Marianne, were both convinced that she had killed him. Fisher's sister and Foyster's relatives came to the same conclusion. During the late 1940s there were even demands for his body to be exhumed for a post-mortem. There is also the possibility that he asked to be put out his misery. He too must have realised that their pension plan, Fisher, had failed, and that their old way of life was at an end. What could Foyster look forward to? If he was cared for by his grand relatives, he would be parted from Marianne. The game was up, the double act was over. It was time to leave the stage. I believe that although Marianne helped him on his way, she might have done this at his own request.

He was buried in Campsea Ashe churchyard, where today his grave is marked by a single stone slab bearing the inscription: 'Lionel Algernon Foyster, Priest. 1878-1945. The Lord is my Shepherd.'

Now Marianne was free to marry her GI sweetheart, whom she later admitted she had never really loved but married out of convenience. Her problem was that she was now forty-six, while O'Neil was only twenty-five. Furthermore, O'Neil's unit was due to be sent to Continental Europe, and she was by no means certain that he would return to her. She therefore put the same plan into operation that she had used with Fisher. She falsely claimed she was pregnant.

The pressures on Marianne to escape from Britain increased during the period immediately after Foyster's death. The long-awaited exposure came when the Suffolk newspapers reported his death and recalled the sensational haunting of Borley. Fisher's sister at last contacted the Misses Bull, who confirmed that Lionel Foyster and Marianne were indeed man and wife. Fisher's sister wrote to Marianne, denouncing her. Marianne replied with delaying tactics, pleading – with utter cynicism – that no action be taken against her for the sake of the children: the same children she was shortly to abandon.

Marianne now entered the most hectic and dangerous period of her life. Her first priority was to marry O'Neil as quickly as possible; US servicemen were supposed to obtain formal permission from the military authorities before marrying a foreigner, but Marianne and O'Neil dispensed with this. They were married slightly less than four months after Foyster's death, at Ipswich Register Office, on 11 August 1945. Eyewitnesses have recalled that O'Neil was late and Marianne was nervous. She appeared to be pregnant, but this was because she had put on weight and had what she called 'a high stomach'.

The certificate shows that Marianne was not only up to her usual tricks but was most anxious to cover her trail. Almost *every* particular on the official document is false: both parties gave false ages (Marianne stated that she was thirty-two and O'Neil that he was twenty-nine), the bride and groom gave the same fictitious address (229 Ranelagh Road which, because of an odd arrangement of side-streets and house numbers, does not exist), Marianne stated that she was the daughter of Shaw Fisher deceased, medical practitioner, and O'Neil said he was an 'engineer's erector' – whatever that is.

At this time, as well as renting the cottage in Rendelsham, Marianne was renting a pied-à-terre in Ranelagh Road from the same Mrs Saunders from whom she'd rented her room in Gyppeswyck Road ten years before, at the start of her Ipswich adventures. The invention of Shaw Fisher, a conflation of her true maiden name (Shaw) and her surname during her bigamous marriage (Fisher) is ingenious. The strangest aspect of the certificate, however, is that there is no indication that O'Neil was an American serviceman. Although his father is stated, correctly, to be V. O'Neil, farmer, deceased, there is no mention of his country of origin. He came to the Register Office in civilian clothes, adding to the subrosa atmosphere of the proceedings.

Marianne and O'Neil had dangerously dispensed with the official US Army bureaucracy, and it is difficult to understand how Marianne thought she could get away with it. Perhaps she was so desperate that any chance was worth taking. She now turned to her other urgent problems: evading Fisher's relatives, especially his sister, proving Foyster's will (of which she was the sole beneficiary and executrix), dispensing with the children she no longer wanted and finding a baby to take with her to America as O'Neil's. The reader will not, I am sure, underestimate either her difficulties or the risks that she was taking. Her response to danger was never surrender but yet more fantastic impostures.

She solved the first problem by vanishing from Dairy Cottage with all the furniture and possessions, and Fisher's car. Fisher was not far behind, but he arrived too late. When he reached Dairy Cottage he found the place empty and Marianne gone – with the children. Adelaide had lived away from home for some time by then, and Astrid was away at boarding school. Fisher broke down completely and vanished into the twilight, under the care of his devoted sister. He lived in the West Country until his death, in the late 1960s, in Worcester. His family decided not to pursue Marianne to spare him further agony.

Marianne had not gone far. She rented a house in Martelsham, 1 Deben Avenue, which was close to another American airbase; this was in late September 1945. She now turned to the problem of finding a baby, correctly deducing that the US authorities would be sympathetic to a woman who had a baby that a GI admitted was his. Help appeared in the form of a woman who really had become pregnant by an American serviceman and whose husband had told her that their marriage could continue only if she disposed of the child. The requirements of this lady and Marianne coincided neatly, and they came to an arrangement; not long after the baby was born in Ipswich on 9 October 1945 Marianne took him as her own and named him Robert Vincent O'Neil. His birth was never registered in the UK either by Marianne or by his natural mother. John Fisher recalls:

After the Easter holidays in 1945 when I returned to school I learned that the Rev. Foyster had died. Later that year we moved to 1 Deben Avenue, Martlesham. I brought a friend home to Deben Avenue by arrangement one Saturday afternoon, but it was obviously inconvenient for us to be there and we were both packed off back to school immediately (St Joseph's R.C. school in Ipswich). On looking back it is obvious that I was not wanted at Deben Avenue. Easter 1946 I was sent to Bramford, near Ipswich, for the holidays.

During one holiday I did spend at Deben Avenue I was confronted with a baby and was told that he was to sleep in my room. He was called Vincent and I cannot recall the name on his ration book except that it began with an A, but it certainly was not Fisher, Foyster or O'Neil and to the best of my knowledge not her child at all. I remember Vincent particularly as he kept me awake at night crying.

In February 1946, while still living at Martelsham, Marianne obtained the probate of Foyster's will, receiving the sum of £850. In May (Whitsun) she solved her final problem, the disposal of the remaining children, her eldest 'son' John and at least one evacuee. The evacuee was easily got rid of by the simple expedient of placing him on a train with a label attached to his coat bearing his name and address, and thus the child travelled back home much in the same manner as he had left it. John was more of a problem, and Marianne hit on another ingenious scheme. During her attendance at the Roman Catholic church in a nearby town, she had made the acquaintance of another Catholic lady. Marianne visited her, casually remarking that she was obliged to go away to Ireland on family business for a few days, and that although she could easily take the baby with her she was unable to take John; would the lady mind looking after him for a short time? The lady agreed. John was left with her and Marianne walked out, according to the lady, just as if she were going out 'to post a letter'. Marianne, of course, was never seen again. According to John:

Some time between Easter and Whitsun 1946 Mrs Fisher took me and a friend to the cinema in ———— and afterwards I was introduced to Mr and Mrs ————. I was told that I would be spending Whitsun half-term with them.

Shortly afterwards I said goodbye to Mrs Fisher (or Mrs O'Neil as she was by then) and she and Vincent (now also called O'Neil) joined Mr O'Neil in America. I never saw her again and was left in the clothes I stood up in with Mr and Mrs ———.

After a few days Mrs ——— became concerned and visited Marianne's address in Martelsham to find the house empty. Neighbours said that the family had suddenly vanished: one day they were there, the next day they were not. The police were approached, and they made a search of sorts, visiting Marianne's old addresses at Rendelsham, Snape and Chillesford, but they drew a blank. Mrs——— initiated her own investigation, employing a local solicitor (C.J. Parry of Wickham Market) who only a few months before had helped Marianne obtain the probate for Foyster's will. Mr Parry was no more successful than the police, which is extraordinary. We can only suppose that he was, for his own reasons, glad that she was out of the way (see p. 148).

Marianne had gone to Tidworth Camp, in Hampshire, where there was a transit centre for 'war brides'. Somehow she got over the US Army bureaucracy (no doubt a babe-in-arms was a great help), in spite of the irregularities of her marriage to O'Neil, who had married without Army permission. Somehow she also overcame the problem of having no birth certificate for (Robert) Vincent. We can only suppose that she achieved this through a combination of her own ability to charm and lie and the confusion and haste with which the US Army was trying to return its personnel and their dependants back to the United States.

Once she was in the transit camp, and processed by the military authorities, she was relatively safe, because the GI brides had few further dealings with the British civil authorities (for example, they no longer held British ration books). She was therefore almost untraceable, and thus eluded the search by the Suffolk police. Marianne claims that before she left England she had a last meeting with the wronged Harry Francis Fisher, during which they talked about the war and little else; and she found time to present herself and baby Robert Vincent to the Roman Catholic priest at St Mary's Axminster, where the child was baptised on 11 July 1946. In August, no doubt with a sigh of relief, she took ship and duly arrived in New York harbour, perhaps the most exotic and mysterious of all 'Eisenhower's Sweethearts'.

14

Epilogue – Main Street USA

Marianne's first home was the O'Neil family farm, which was in the Mississippi bluff country of Minnesota, a few miles outside the small town of Hokah on Highway 44. O'Neil's father had died some years before, and his mother, Esther, and grandmother lived there with the rest of the family. They had never made more than the barest living from the farm. Hokah today is much the same as it was when Marianne first saw it, and the town could have sprung from the pages of Sinclair Lewis's classic tale of small-town America, *Main Street*. Marianne perhaps suffered the disillusionment of many GI brides when their expansive, wealthy and victorious husbands took them home.

By a curious coincidence, I not only know Borley well but also Hokah and other American towns in which Marianne settled. Hokah is not far from La Crosse, where Marianne now lives. La Crosse is a substantial town on the Wisconsin side of the Mississippi. Minneapolis is about 100 miles north-west. To the west there is nothing but an endless succession of small towns, and the pleasant wooded bluff country soon gives way to the prairies which roll on to the Rockies. The climate is severe – by British standards at least – with very hot summers and very cold winters marked by frequent blizzards that cut off smaller communities for days. Marianne arrived in this alien environment to find that, if she had not already guessed it, her GI husband was a work-shy drunkard and completely unreliable.

When she was re-united with him, after travelling by train from New York, she found that he was unemployed and determined to remain so. At first they lived on capital, a major part of which was presumably the £850 left to Marianne by Foyster. They moved out of the farm into a small wooden house in Hokah and bought a car. It was destroyed in an accident on Highway 44 while being driven by a man named Sauer, the nephew of the Hokah barber. O'Neil was a passenger and was quite badly hurt, suffering a fractured jaw. Marianne wrote to her friend in Wimbledon, Mrs Fenton, pathetically recounting how *she* (not O'Neil) had been in an auto smash and of how *her* jaw had been fractured. This pointless piece of romancing is interesting because it demonstrates how Marianne simply could not tell the truth. Most of her lies were fantasy, not falsehoods told to manipulate others. She had not even been in the car when it crashed.

Because O'Neil showed no desire to earn a living, Marianne was obliged to find a job. The couple gained the reputation of bad credit risks after they had defaulted on bills owing to several local stores. For a while Marianne worked for a local newspaper, the *Hokah Chief*, and then (in about 1949) at the prairie school near Bangor in Wisconsin, on the other side of the river. The prairie schools were originally small, one-room schoolhouses, built to bring rudimentary education to outlying communities. They were already a dying institution in Marianne's day, and she hastened their decline by being a quite incompetent teacher. To obtain the job she had claimed that she was a graduate of the University of London, and that she had had teaching experience in Canada and elsewhere.

Marianne's American story (to which she has stuck more or less consistently for over forty years) is that she was the daughter of a successful doctor from Maine, named Fisher, that she had served with the US forces in Europe during the war and that she lost a brother in combat. Again, we see how she weaves details of her history into her fantasies; she had lived near the border of Maine and New Brunswick with Foyster during their Canadian days and knew enough about the region to flesh out her story with circumstantial detail.

Marianne's marriage with O'Neil ran into trouble. O'Neil left Hokah with a woman named Beverly St Jacques, and (Robert) Vincent was placed for a short while in a children's home in La Crosse. Marianne was obliged to look for work again, and found a job as a reporter for the *Jamestown Sun*, the local newspaper of Jamestown, North Dakota. She duly took herself to Jamestown, and after a short delay she was joined by (Robert) Vincent. A reconciliation with O'Neil took place, for he too joined her and obtained work as a plumber. Unfortunately his career as a plumber was blighted by his general dislike of work and his heavy drinking. Marianne ended up supporting not only the child, but also her hopeless husband, on a meagre salary of $45 per week.

Marianne clearly regarded men with utter contempt, founded in part perhaps on her discovery of the ease with which they could be persuaded to satisfy her sexual needs; and yet she seems never to have had relationships with men who were *not* contemptible figures, with the possible exception of the enigmatic and wonderful Santiago Monk. O'Neil was a drunken bum, Fisher had been a mentally unstable commercial traveller, Davies had been driven to the limits of his sanity by grief for his dead wife and could only have sex by indulging in the fiction that he was embracing not Marianne but Tweatie, Edwin Whitehouse was greatly exercised by whether he should devote his life to Spiritualism or become a Roman Catholic priest and saw things flying round his head, d'Arles (or Pearless) was a violent lout off the London streets, and Lionel Algernon Foyster defies brief description. It is odd that not even once did Marianne, a woman of great charm and attractiveness, have a relationship with a decent man with whom she was really in love. We must remember that she had no close female friends to console her in her loneliness, and that she was cruel, violent and callous towards her children. Her whole personality exhibits a curious detachment, and in spite of her fantasies she seems to have been quite unaware of what she might achieve through a more productive use of her extraordinary abilities. Behind the grace and wit and charm, she seems emotionally atrophied. It is as if there isn't a whole person there; and this is a characteristic of many adults who have, during their childhood, suffered sexual abuse from adults. One thinks of the close relationship that developed between the little Marianne who loved to pretend that she was a princess and the curate of Oughtrington. Perhaps, if Marianne had suffered such abuse during her childhood, her attitude to men would have been a combination of pathetic dependence for reassurance that she was wanted and pleasing, and a fierce hatred and contempt; the most celebrated example of such a character is the Twenties film star Louise Brooks, whose life had been altered by a childhood encounter with a man named Mr Flowers.

*

In Jamestown Marianne was well-liked and was good at her job. I have talked to several people who knew and worked with her; there was no hint of scandal. No one remembered the drunken husband at all. He seems to have kept his head down. She did a bit of Munchausening by enthralling the Jamestown ladies' club with her dramatic first-hand accounts of the perils of the London Blitz. The reader will remember, of course, that during the Blitz she was living in rural Suffolk, and that her trips to London involved not hair's-breadth escapes but trances in the lounge of the Grosvenor Hotel. She also stuck to her story about being the daughter of a doctor from Maine.

Marianne had left such a confused trail behind her that in Jamestown she felt relatively safe. Jamestown is, after all, a long way from anywhere else. The nearest towns of any size are Fargo 90 miles to the east, where, on the North Dakota-Minnesota border the railroad crosses the Red River, and the state capital, Bismarck (named after the German Chancellor by the railroad pioneers in the hope of attracting German investment) 100 miles to the west. Unfortunately for her, Trevor Hall was on her trail back in England; and in February 1958 A. Robert Swanson, Investigator, knocked on her door, which was answered by her husband, the former GI. He was described by Swanson as a man of medium height and build, and with slightly reddish hair and several days' growth of beard.

Marianne was still at work, but when she came back, Swanson introduced himself and, when O'Neil was out of the room, explained his business.

Marianne's son Ian, who had himself approached Hall after the publication of the *Haunting of Borley Rectory*, had already written to her to warn her that she was being tracked. None the less the arrival of a tough American private investigator in the arctic snows of Jamestown gave her an unpleasant shock. At first she refused to discuss anything with Swanson, but she later relented and, at the Gladstone Hotel, Jamestown, gave the interviews (tape-recorded by Swanson) which have been extensively quoted throughout this book.

Although Ian warned Marianne that the hunt was afoot, it was through him that Hall learned her address. Ian regarded his mother with loathing and contempt, and was incapable of saying anything good of her. For this reason his statements about her must be treated with some caution, especially since most of them are impossible to corroborate. After living at Wimbledon with Marianne and d'Arles, above the flower shop, he had gone back to Northern Ireland to live with his grandparents. He returned to London in 1942 to work on bomb-site clearance and remained there. Hall talked to him at length, and Ian provided much of the material quoted in this book. He was shocked to learn of the Fisher marriage, for he had been in Ireland during the time of Marianne's Ipswich escapades.

Hall contacted Marianne using Ian as an intermediary. Marianne, realising that the game in England was up, promptly denied that she had had any part in haunting Borley and threatened suicide. Hall was obliged to write to her assuring her that he meant her no harm, and that there was no need to use the gun she said lay before her on the table. What he did not tell her was that he had initiated an investigation in the United States, in collaboration with the Parapsychological Foundation of New York, which was run by the famous medium (with whom Hall later fell out) Mrs Eileen Garrett. The Foundation in turn hired Swanson, and Swanson followed Marianne's trail right up to her door in Jamestown.

Marianne gave Swanson the much-quoted interview when she was caught off-guard and therefore likely to tell the truth. I am inclined to believe statements made in this interview rather than later ones that are thought out and calculated. None the less an examination of the transcript shows that Marianne was trying to lie even at this stage. Only when Swanson produced a mass of documentary evidence that she could not deny did she give an approximation to the truth. Yet her replies were always self-exculpatory, and where possible she blamed everyone else for what had happened. Foyster was off his rocker, Mrs Fenton of Wimbledon should have told her to stop telling fairy-tales, d'Arles and Price were responsible for Borley and so on. Only someone with an encyclopaedic knowledge of her past could have pinned her down; which Swanson had, and did.

Marianne was persuaded to fly to New York in May 1958 to visit the Parapsychological Foundation. Here she gave more interviews, told a few more lies and was caught out, was taken out to dinner and returned intact to Jamestown. She was very anxious that she might be deported – as indeed she could have been – if the American immigration authorities learned that the baby was not really hers or O'Neil's and that she had entered the US under false pretences. Swanson and Mrs Garrett recorded their impressions of Marianne as follows:

Swanson says she has no mean opinion of herself. She identifies with Rita Hayworth, remarking that just as Rita Hayworth has had many husbands, so has she, Marianne.
Swanson feels very strongly that there must be something in her background ... He feels that as soon as he got her to break down, she did reveal actual fear and much agitation lest she should be deported to England ... He enquires whether Mr Hall has reason to believe that there is something in her background as yet unrevealed ... Swanson admitted to Mr Ebon that if he had stayed around Marianne much longer, she most certainly would have made a pitch for him ... We ought to hold this in mind in case you have need of his services where Marianne is concerned in the future!

Marianne had declined since her glory days in England. She was, after all, 59 when Swanson appeared at her door. A summary of Swanson's experiences includes the following, which will no doubt enrage feminist readers:

Marianne O'Neil is not attractive from a physical standpoint. She does not have a slim figure but is inclined to look heavy and out of shape. Her hair is reddish and in need of work by a beautician but her hair was neat from home care. Her clothes are inexpensive although neat. She earns take-home pay of $45 per week. Her husband is a drunkard and seldom works ...

Mrs Garrett's impressions of Marianne, when she met her in New York:

Marianne laughs easily and has a quite beguiling personality once she is off her guard, and quite unblushingly told Mr Swanson that she had every intention of lying to him, and I fear she will do it again since for her lying is like a game ... She was amusing, gay all through dinner. I pressed the bottle close to her, she drank like a lady and showed no visible or outside signs of being affected by it. She talked intelligently about a book she is writing and we suggested to her that she should write a book about the whole Borley experience ... Apart from the seriousness of the subject I was frankly amused by her, and I can readily see that she is willing to enter into any form of mischief. I asked her point blank whether she had killed Foyster. She answered equally candidly that it had often been in her mind, but that he was too cunning for anything like that to happen to him. Again and again she remarked that he lay in bed and wrote all kinds of imaginative stories which were to be presented about Borley ... I feel sorry for her in spite of her wilfulness and mischievousness ...

Finally, we note that Swanson had the distinct impression

that Marianne did in fact murder Foyster, and that the memory of this greatly disturbed her.

The whole investigation greatly disturbed her too, and although she enjoyed her free trip to New York she felt uneasy in Jamestown. She feared that her past would become known there. Therefore, though she liked her job and the town, she moved in the autumn of 1958 to Fargo, a much larger place, and obtained a job as a 'Special Instructor' at North Dakota Agricultural College. Sadly, I found that no one at this institution remembers her now, and I was unable to find out exactly what her duties were.

She moved every year thereafter, presumably to keep other investigators at some distance; the street directories of Fargo list her as living at 1120 South 13th Street, with her son Vincent aged 13 in 1959, and then at 1325 South 8th Street in 1960. In 1961 she is listed as the widow of Robert O'Neil, living at 1126 4th Avenue South. Now she was a case worker for the Lutheran Welfare Society.

I visited this institution, where she was remembered. She had worked on a welfare programme which organised the adoption of babies of 'unwedded mothers' and had been very good at what she did. Everyone who remembered her spoke of her with great affection. There was no hint of poltergeists or scandals.

She moved again, in 1962 and 1963, and in that year left Fargo for good, going to La Crosse in Wisconsin where she has been ever since. No one to whom I spoke had the faintest idea that when they knew her she was already in her late fifties. The following remarks are typical.

'Marianne O'Neil? Oh yes, I remember her, she'd be about retiring age now.'

'She was always kind of young and flamboyant, you know?'

'She always wore this bright red lipstick and had this white skin. Oh, and she always wore these low-cut dresses.'

'The last time I saw her was in Fargo, she was propping up the VFW bar and looked like she was having a lot of fun.'

The description of Marianne as a widow in several of the entries of the street directory is wrong. She divorced O'Neil in 1959 but later allowed him to live with her because he was such a hopeless case, unable to support himself and disowned by his family in Hokah. This is in striking contrast to her treatment of other men apart from Foyster. O'Neil was always in debt because of his drinking and his refusal to work, and Marianne's description of herself as a widow was presumably to afford both of them some protection against credit agencies.

In La Crosse Marianne was again involved with social work and had a highly successful career; the project of which she was a co-founder received state (i.e. from the State of Wisconsin) recognition and funding, and she has become a highly respected pillar of the community. She was still working in the mid-Eighties!

Marianne's life in America spans 45 years, and in that time, although she has continued her romancing on a limited scale (she now describes herself as the widow of Captain O'Neil), there have been no impostures or escapades of the sort she practised in England. She was devoted to her son, (Robert) Vincent, and they have lived together for many years. There is, therefore, an obvious discontinuity between her behaviour in England and her behaviour in the United States.

Her desperate situation in the years before her departure from England must have taught her a bitter lesson; and Hall's investigation was unpleasant and threatening, leaving her with the feeling that for ever afterwards she was being watched – which she was. Her adventures at Borley have made her a cult figure for psychical researchers, and she must have learned that what, in her own words, 'starts off as a bit of harmless fun' can have terrible consequences for its perpetrator. Furthermore, although she always looked much younger than she really was, she must have begun to feel her age not long after she arrived in the United States. The false age on her marriage certificate obliged her to pretend to be fourteen years younger than she really was thereafter.

Her career in La Crosse, and her resourcefulness in overcoming the problem of being in a strange country with a drunken, work-shy husband, confirm what most people would suspect from reading her life-story: that she was a remarkably talented and gifted woman. She came close to self-destruction through her pathological dependence on men. Perhaps the real villain of the piece is that deeply religious and saintly cleric, Lionel Algernon Foyster, whose response to his wife's character was to assist her to sink into the depths with men such as d'Arles, and who used her sexual abnormalities for vicarious gratification.

I have often remarked that Marianne had no intimate friends; the exception to this would appear to be Foyster, for, as I hope I have shown in this book, Marianne's activities would have been impossible without his full cooperation. That Foyster was a corrupting influence on her is indicated by her transformation when she was at last free of him and in another country.

Marianne should be allowed the last words. In 1958 she wrote to Robert Swanson:

I hoped that I had heard the last of that other life, in another country, in another world. What more can I add? After all it is twenty years ago and I am not the person I was. You may not believe it but it is true.

All that I ask is just to be left in peace to live out the rest of my life in quiet decency and in the serenity of the American way of life. I have friends, I have my child, my work, here in America, life is good and above all, I pray that no hurt through me will ever come to Vincent, and the many folks here.

Marianne

Bibliography

Life of Harry Price and background:

Hall, T.H., *The Search for Harry Price*, Duckworth (1978)
Tabori, P., *Harry Price: The Biography of a Ghost Hunter*, Athenaeum (1950), Sphere (1974)
Price, H., *Search for Truth*, Collins (1942)
   Fifty Years of Psychical Research, Longman (1939)
   The Haunting of Cashens Gap, Methuen (1936)

The haunting of Borley:

Dingwall, E.J., Goldney, K.M., Hall, T.H., *The Haunting of Borley Rectory*, Duckworth (1956)
Hall, T.H., *New Light on Old Ghosts*, Duckworth (1965)
Hastings, R.J., *Reply to the Borley Report*, Proc. SPR (1969), *51*, 1-180
Owen, I.M., Mitchell, P., *The Alleged Haunting of Borley Rectory*, Journal of SPR (1979) *50*, 149-62
Price, H., *The Most Haunted House in England*, Longman (1940), Time-Life (1990)
   The End of Borley Rectory, Harrap (1946), Cedric-Chivers/Library Assoc. (1975)
Underwood, P., *Hauntings*, Dent (1975)
Underwood, P., Tabori, P. *The Ghosts of Borley*, David and Charles (1973)

Index